Key Topics in Quantitative Research

This book gives an overview of the key topics in quantitative methods. Written by an academic who has specialised in quantitative methods in Psychology across a range of sub disciplines, it highlights how crucial understanding quantitative methods is to understanding research in psychology and beyond.

First, it briefly considers the history of quantitative methods in psychology citing some key figures in both psychology and statistics. Following this, it will describe how we apply models of scientific investigation in psychology to generate reliable knowledge. It will then go on to consider key models we use in quantitative research, from experimental designs to quasi-experimental and correlational designs. Next, it introduces sampling theory, and its role in understanding who our findings apply to. The final theoretical consideration is a concise description of null hypothesis significance testing and how we can use it to make inferences about psychological phenomena. In the next part of the book, there will be a focus on some core methods, starting with a discussion of how we sample participants before exploring statistics in detail. Next, the book looks at how robust quantitative research can impact other fields and policy through improving ecological validity and reliability. Finally, the book gets to grips with key challenges in the future of quantitative research with a discussion of the replication crisis and solutions to it, and then explores how we can improve inclusivity.

This book is an essential text for all students of quantitative methodology.

Paul Christiansen is a professor of applied statistics at the Department of Psychology in University of Liverpool. He is interested in research integrity with a particular focus on accurate measurement (psychometrics). He works across a range of fields in Psychology (appetite and obesity, addiction, forensic, and health psychology) as well as medical research.

BPS Key Topics Series

British Psychological Society

Routledge, in partnership with the British Psychological Society (BPS), is pleased to present *BPS Key Topics in Psychology*, a series of short introductory books that focus on a specific field within psychology. Each book is broken down into bitesize chunks to provide a helpful overview of core psychology topics, made clear by a five-part structure: foundations, theories, methodologies, impacts, and emerging areas. Written by active and experienced authors, these essential books encourage students to approach fundamental concepts with confidence and critical thinking.

Books may incorporate student-friendly pedagogies, including tools such as: feature boxes; key terms and definitions; and links to further reading online. Concise yet comprehensive, these books offer a simple and accessible overview of core psychology topics for students looking for a summary of key concepts in the topic, or those new to the area.

Key Topics in Coaching Psychology
Rebecca J. Jones and Holly Andrews

Key Topics in Quantitative Research
Paul Christiansen

Key Topics in Educational Psychology
Lisa Marks Woolfson

For more information about this series, please visit: www.routledge.com/ BPS-Key-Topics-in-Psychology/book-series/BPSKTP

Key Topics in Quantitative Research

Paul Christiansen

Routledge
Taylor & Francis Group

LONDON AND NEW YORK

the british
psychological society
accredited undergraduate psychology

Designed cover image: Getty images via denkcreative

First published 2025
by Routledge
4 Park Square, Milton Park, Abingdon, Oxon OX14 4RN

and by Routledge
605 Third Avenue, New York, NY 10158

Routledge is an imprint of the Taylor & Francis Group, an informa business

© 2025 Paul Christiansen

The right of Paul Christiansen to be identified as author of this work has been asserted in accordance with sections 77 and 78 of the Copyright, Designs and Patents Act 1988.

All rights reserved. No part of this book may be reprinted or reproduced or utilised in any form or by any electronic, mechanical, or other means, now known or hereafter invented, including photocopying and recording, or in any information storage or retrieval system, without permission in writing from the publishers.

Trademark notice: Product or corporate names may be trademarks or registered trademarks, and are used only for identification and explanation without intent to infringe.

Access the Support Material: www.routledge.com/9781032612386

British Library Cataloguing-in-Publication Data
A catalogue record for this book is available from the British Library

ISBN: 978-1-032-65653-3 (hbk)
ISBN: 978-1-032-61238-6 (pbk)
ISBN: 978-1-032-65656-4 (ebk)

DOI: 10.4324/9781032656564

Typeset in Galliard
by Taylor & Francis Books

Contents

Figures

Tables

Boxes

Section 1

Key Foundations

This section aims to set the scene for quantitative methods, describing why it is so critical to your studies before moving on to some historical context. Then it will discuss the theoretical underpinnings of the scientific method and, finally, the properties of different types of numeric data.

At the end of Section 1, you will:

1.1 Know why understanding quantitative methods will make you an all-around better student.
1.2 Have learned about the early pioneers in the field, appreciating how far we have come in such a short time.
1.3 Gain knowledge of the general scientific process and how we convert psychological phenomena to numerical outputs so we can treat psychology as a science.
1.4 Understand the different types of numerical data we can collect and their properties.

DOI: 10.4324/9781032656564-1

Chapter 1

Introduction

Introduction

This book aims to familiarise you with the core concepts of quantitative research. I am sure few of you have decided to do an undergraduate psychology degree because you really wanted to learn about quantitative methods, and probably even fewer of you have chosen to do a psychology degree because you are interested in statistics. Indeed, these two things were low on my list of reasons for doing a psychology degree too. However, over the years working across multiple fields in psychology, I came to understand that if you know quantitative methods, you are better placed to understand research no matter what the subject is.

Over the coming years, you will see how vital quantitative methods are to psychology, indeed the majority of things that you will learn about will be viewed through the lens of quantitative methods. This book will give you an excellent understanding of the core concepts of quantitative research, building a strong foundation for your studies.

This book will be split into sub-sections and within these, there will be chapters that will focus on one core theme with clear learning outcomes for each sub-section:

Section 1 Key Foundations: This will set the scene for quantitative methods, describing why they are so critical to your studies before moving on to some historical context. Then it will discuss the theoretical underpinnings of the scientific method and, finally, the properties of different types of numeric data.

Section 2 Key Theories: This will focus on the building blocks of designing and understanding quantitative studies. This will then be mapped onto sampling methods, before finally addressing the core statistical concept that is statistical significance.

DOI: 10.4324/9781032656564-2

Section 3 Key Methodologies: Section 3 moves on to some practicalities of quantitative methods, looking at sampling methods before giving an overview of statistical tests.

Section 4 Key Impacts on Research or Practice and Policy: This section will focus on using optimal quantitative methods so that findings can be reliably translated to the real world.

Section 5 Key Emerging Areas – where is the research headed? The final section will look at recent developments and controversies in quantitative methods.

Why should I read this book?

For quantitative methods modules

Quantitative methods are going to take up a significant proportion of your teaching time. You will no doubt have assessments specifically on quantitative methods, so having a good understanding of the basics will mean that you will be able to get the most out of your classes and perform well. Notably, some students have a fear of quantitative methods as they don't view themselves as "maths people", indeed there is a term for this: Statistics Anxiety. This fear is often unfounded; indeed myself and colleagues (Hunt et al., 2023) found that statistics anxiety was associated with students *predicting* they would get poor grades, but also associated with *improved* exam performance! Hopefully, by reading this book you will become less worried about quantitative methods and more confident in your ability.

For your final year project

This book will not only help with modules focused on quantitative methods. As part of your undergraduate degree, you will do a research project (or dissertation) in your final year. This is where you will do some research; designing the study, collecting and analysing data, and writing it all up. If you do a quantitative project at all of these stages you are going to need the knowledge you have gained from this book.

For every other module that you do!

If that hasn't convinced you to read this book cover to cover, I think this will. Knowledge of psychology comes from reading research. Over the coming years, you are going to read a lot of scientific papers. If you hope to understand what they are doing, why they are doing it, and the findings, then understanding quantitative methods is essential. Indeed, an elevated understanding of quantitative methods will allow you to engage with research at a much higher level, improving your assessment grades significantly.

Moreover, it will allow you to spot problems with research; throughout this book, I will be pointing out common problems in research. Now, you may find it surprising that there is research out there that has fundamental flaws in it, surely scientists know what they are doing right? Well, unfortunately, they often do not – and this is often a product of their lack of knowledge of quantitative methods! There are many examples of bad quantitative methods that have been proven to give poor results but keep getting used. If you can recognise these problems then you will be able to effectively critically appraise research, which is something that will make your work stand out.

Indeed, try to avoid the mindset where you put different subjects into separate silos. What you learn in one module may contribute to an understanding of another module, and few areas will cross over as much as quantitative methods. View it as a key basis for your understanding of psychology as a whole and you will get so much more out of your degree.

For the rest of your life

Finally, having a good understanding of quantitative methods is a really important life skill. Employers are often interested in potential employees who have excellent quantitative skills, indeed around 70% of employers say quantitative skills are important or essential to them (Mason, Nathan & Rosso, 2015). Being able to handle data, understand effective measurement, and the role data has in evidencing best practice is therefore a must in many jobs, not just those directly related to psychology. Indeed with "big data" driving so many decisions across workplaces the knowledge you gain from this book may well have lifelong benefits.

Finally, you will be able to see through pop science "influencers" and the hyperbole in newspaper headlines, making you less susceptible to believing the nonsense that pervades traditional and social media!

Conclusion

Hopefully, I have convinced you of just how essential quantitative methods are going to be. I promise you that it is nothing to be fearful of and the knowledge you gain from this book will help you in your study of quantitative methods and beyond. I may be biased here, but I really think that this book will be invaluable to you as you negotiate your way through your entire undergraduate degree, and by reading this you will set yourself up for a successful degree and future career.

References

Hunt, B. W., Mari, T., Knibb, G., Christiansen, P., & Jones, A. (2023). *Statistics anxiety and predictions of exam performance in UK psychology students*. PloS one, 18(8), e0290467.

Mason, G., Nathan, M. and Rosso, A. (2015). *State of the Nation: A review of evidence on the supply and demand of quantitative skills*. British Academy & NIESR.

Chapter 2

Key Early figures in Quantitative Methods

Introduction

Psychology is a relatively new science. Although people explored "psychology" for many years before the term became commonplace, it was not necessarily done with the scientific rigour it is today. Indeed, there is a long history of attempting to understand behaviour, thoughts, perceptions etc, although this was done from a philosophical or theological perspective. We can look back as far as Aristotle's (384–322 BC) works of De Anima and Parava Naturalia, in which psychology is seen as part of broader investigations into the soul. Over the years many philosophers grappled with psychological processes, for example, Thomas Hobbes, John Locke, and Arthur Schopenhauer, attempted to understand how the human mind interacts with the wider world and the biological processes of the body. However, none of these can be seen as bringing quantitative methods into psychology. I would argue that pinning down one individual as the *originator of quantitative methods* in the study of psychological phenomena is a near-impossible task with scholars suggesting giving the title to a range of individuals, all for good reason.

What is apparent though is that the earliest examples of quantitative methods in psychology are largely focused on human perception, and as such are hard to distinguish from the field of psychophysics (the study of sensory processes and limitations through observing behaviour in response to sensory stimuli). It could be argued that this field gave rise to modern quantitative psychology.

Psychophysics and psychological processes

Psychophysics was a term first used by Gustav Fechner in 1860, (more on him in a moment) which he described in "Psychophysik" as "*an exact science of the functional or*

> **Psychophysics.** The study of the relationship between physical stimuli and the sensory/perceptual experiences they generate.

DOI: 10.4324/9781032656564-3

dependence relationships between bodies and souls, or more generally between the material and spiritual, the physical and psychical worlds". **The latter part of this definition is particularly useful – the relationship between the physical and psychical world, i.e. how environmental stimuli interact with our perceptual systems.** Although this is the first time we see psychophysics explicitly described, it is possible to argue that the field predates it by a significant degree.

Hasan Ibn al-Haytham (965–1040)

Ibn al-Haytham was born in modern-day Iraq in Basra, although much of his famous work comes from his years in Egypt. Although he was a polymath, writing on mathematics, engineering, and medicine, he can be argued to be one of the founders of modern psychology, using experimental methodologies to study optics. Indeed, he correctly argued that the eyes sense light from objects and that we perceive in the brain, not the eyes. Moreover, he was particularly interested in studying errors in vision and using these to build an understanding of visual perception. Throughout his work "Optics", he makes clear statements about using experimental methods to study perception, using clearly defined measurements and apparatus. Although perhaps not a quantitative psychologist *per se*, it is clear that he is one of the originators of using robust scientific methods to study psychological phenomena. This makes him an important progenitor of the field. For more reading on Ibn al-Haytham see Khaleefa (1999).

Gustav Fechner (1801–1887)

Gustav Fechner was born in Gross Särchen in Germany, and worked largely in Leipzig. He is often considered the founder of psychophysics. Fechner used quantitative methods to study the relationship between physical stimuli and perceptual experiences. "Elements of Psychophysics" (1860) established methods to measure sensory thresholds and introduced Weber-Fechner law, which argues that the perceived perceptual properties (visual or auditory) of stimuli are proportional to their actual intensity (as measured by a scientific instrument).

Moreover, Fechner developed three methods for studying threshold responses to stimuli:

Method of limits: Stimuli are presented and then increased in intensity in predetermined steps until an individual can perceive it at 50% of presentations (the absolute threshold of determination). This can be repeated, and done in ascending or descending intensity.

Method of adjustment: Participants are given control over stimuli which they adjust until they can only just perceive it. This is repeated several times with the mean intensity being the participants' threshold.

Method of constant stimuli: In this, a range of stimuli are presented, some which the experimenter believes can be perceived, some which they believe cannot be perceived, and some in between. These are presented in a random order and the participant will state whether they can be perceived or not.

In Table 2.1 the method of limits is demonstrated; a participant listens to sounds at different frequencies that the experimenter increases or decreases in units of two Hertz (Hz). The participant states when they can hear the sound (at which point the experimenter stops).

Set one threshold = 18hz, set two =20hz, set three = 18hz and set four 20hz; this gives an average absolute threshold of 19.625hz.

This method takes a subjective experience of hearing sound in a controlled environment and, using calibrated equipment, produces a quantitative measure of this perception (i.e. assigns a numerical value to it).

Using these methods Fechner was able to operationalise psychological processes that have no true unit of measurement (we cannot have a universal perception value across people as people differ) so they can be studied in a scientific (and quantitative) manner. Indeed, his quote *"As an exact science psychophysics, like physics, must rest on experience and the mathematical connection of those empirical facts that demand a measure of what is experienced or, when such a measure is not available, a search for it."* shows how Fechner was attempting to make psychological processes grounded in mathematical rules.

Table 2.1 Collecting data using the method of limits

Sound frequency	Set 1 (increasing)	Set 2 (decreasing)	Set 3 (increasing)	Set 4 (decreasing)
28hz		√		√
26hz		√		√
24hz		√		√
22hz		√		√
20hz		√	√	√
18hz	√	x	x	x
16hz	x		x	
14hz	x		x	
12hz	x		x	
10hz	x		x	

Intelligence

Another field in which we first see early quantitative psychology is the study of intelligence. As you will see, although some innovative methods were used, some of their findings are highly problematic and flawed. For a detailed discussion of intelligence testing see Curtis and Glaser (1981).

Francis Galton (1822–1911)

Francis Galton (born in Birmingham, UK) was a polymath who was especially interested in the hereditary nature of traits, particularly intelligence. He was the originator of using standardised questions i.e. formal questionnaires; realising that by asking specific questions and aggregating responses, he would be able to conduct statistical analysis of responses. In "English Men of Science-Their Nature and Nurture" he reported the product of giving ~200 preeminent English scientists formal questionnaires to understand the extent to which their abilities were the product of hereditary and environmental influences, concluding that much of intelligence was hereditary and society to be structured according to this.

These conclusions led to the development of the now-discredited Eugenics, which advocated that selective breeding could increase intelligence. Indeed, much of this movement's conclusions were based upon an erroneous understanding of intelligence and the extent to which it is hereditary. The arguments made by this movement resulted in conclusions that some races were inferior and unable to achieve levels of intelligence that were seen in white Europeans. Furthermore, Galton had a firm belief that head size was correlated with intelligence. When one of his disciples, Karl Pearson, tested this idea, he found that the association between head size and intelligence was weak. This caused Galton some consternation "*The non-correlation of ability and size of the head continues to puzzle me the more I recall my own measurement and observations of the most eminent men of the day*" (Pearson, 1930). It is notable he also believed intelligence could be measured through a range of what we would see as physical tests such as reaction time.

Galton was the originator of many statistical terms that we still use today. For example, median (midpoint of a distribution), percentile, and regression to the mean (we will discuss this later). This is quite a substantive influence, so although many of his views are extremely distasteful, it is hard to argue that he was not a big influence on the field of quantitative methods.

James McKeen Cattell (1860–1944)

Cattell brought the ideas of Galton to the US. He devised a series of tests that were aimed at assessing intelligence (based on the erroneous theories of Galton; see Cattell 1890). These included the strength of someone's grip, the fastest movement of a hand across 50cm, and the least noticeable difference in weights (holding boxes of different weights and saying which was heavier). Although we may ask, "What the hell were they thinking?" This is still an attempt to quantify high-order psychological functioning using standardised methods to give a value i.e. an intelligence score. Problematically one of Cattell's students found that test performance did not correlate with grades!

Alfred Binet (1857–1911)

The fundamental issues with Galton's theory, shown in Cattell's experiments, highlighted the failures of these methods to test intelligence. Alfred Binet (born in Nice, France) developed a multifactorial version of intelligence testing. Using standardised testing techniques, he, along with Theophile Simon, developed the Binet-Simon scale (1908, 1911). This measured a range of things including problem-solving and perception, and produced the intelligence quotient score (IQ) which is standardised across ages. Variations of this scale are still used, although the original form is now very dated and requires cultural knowledge.

Charles Spearman (1863–1945):

Spearman trained under Wilhelm Wundt (see below). Spearman proposed the concept of the "g" factor (general intelligence) and developed methods to measure it. He also was a key figure in the development of the statistical method called factor analysis as well as the Spearman rank correlation. Indeed, Spearman's work is an excellent example of how the new field of psychology demanded new quantitative methods.

Psychology as a field of study

We can see over the two examples of Psychophysics and Intelligence testing the beginnings of quantitative psychology. There are, however, some key figures in the development of what we would recognise as more modern quantitative psychology. Here are three that I think are particularly important.

Wilhelm Wundt (1832–1920)

Born in Mannheim in Germany, and working for much of his career in Leipzig, Wundt is one of the first true psychologists since he made a clear distinction between psychology, philosophy, and biology. He set up the first experimental psychology laboratories. Although much of his work involved introspection, he attempted to do this rigorously: those doing introspection had to be highly trained and had to do it under controlled conditions enabling them to do it systematically. It is this latter point that makes him so important; he emphasized precise control over conditions to focus on phenomena. Even if we now see methods of introspection as the antithesis of quantitative psychology it should be appreciated how he attempted to bring rigour to this process.

Wundt did develop what we would recognise as modern quantitative methods as well. He pioneered reaction time experiments, for example, he would present subjects with a light and then measure how long it took them to respond to it. Some of his work on memory was also more like a modern psychology experiment. For example, he presented letters in a circle around a fixation point; participants were then exposed to the letters very briefly and then had to report how many letters they saw (see Carpenter, 2005 for more descriptions of Wundt's experiments).

Through varying task complexity or conditions, he attempted to understand the mental substrates of cognitive processes which he believed to be irreducible. He argued that these psychical elements were combined to give rise to more intricate processes such as emotion.

The (often) scientific approach used by Wundt and his many students and colleagues in their research means that he is commonly referred to as the father of modern psychology. Indeed, he was one of the first to refer to himself as a psychologist and to set up a dedicated psychology laboratory.

Hermann Ebbinghaus (1850–1909)

Ebbinghaus conducted the first quantitative studies of memory. His experiments using nonsense syllables led to him producing the forgetting curve and discovering the spacing effect, which are still fundamental principles in the study of memory, which he described in "Memory: A Contribution to Experimental Psychology" (1885). With the forgetting curve, Ebbinghaus demonstrated how memory declines over time; again this may seem obvious to us but this is the first time the process was quantitatively demonstrated using robust methods. Critically, Murre and Dros (2015) largely replicated his findings showing how robust the quantitative methods Ebbinghaus employed produced consistent findings.

One of Ebbinghaus' most noticeable influences is how we write up studies using quantitative methods. He is responsible for the research report standardisation that we use today with sections of Introduction, Methods, Results, and Discussion.

Beatrice Edgell (1871–1948)

Born in Tewkesbury, Gloucestershire, Beatrice Edgell was the first British female to receive a PhD (*"The limits of the experiment as a psychological method"*), she was also the first female head of the BPS. She made a significant contribution to quantitative methods and was a driving force behind psychology being seen as a hard science. She conducted research in a range of fields. For example, she completed numerous studies into time perception, in which she searched for an "indifference point" a length of time that is not over nor underestimated. In these studies, participants were given a range of time intervals that they had to estimate, with multiple trials across participants. Then in another study participants were given two intervals (long and short) and then had to estimate a mid-point, with the long to short intervals varying. Here we can see how different quantitative methods are being used to understand a single psychological phenomenon.

She was also technically gifted, improving the accuracy of the Wheatstone-Hipp chronoscope (a device for measuring time). This showed an appreciation of the role that accurate measurement has in assessing psychological processes – if you want to study something, measure it in the best way possible. Although not one of the most famous of the early psychologists, her influence was huge and she is one of the most important early thinkers in quantitative methods.

Statisticians

We could go back a long way in the study of statistics, I have just highlighted some of those that have been (and still are) particularly influential in quantitative methods in psychology, (don't forget that Galton was also an early progenitor of modern statistics as well).

Karl Pearson (1857–1936)

As mentioned earlier, Karl Pearson was a statistician who researched eugenics. He was incredibly important to the field of statistics, and you will no doubt be using some of the tests he derived over the coming years, namely the Pearson's correlation and the Pearson Chi-Squared test (clearly, he was not one for modesty).

Ronald Fisher (1890–1962)

Often seen as a founding figure of modern statistics, Fisher was another polymath working across fields. He is responsible for what we see as the threshold of statistical significance (a probability of less than .05, i.e. less than 5%; for details on this see Chapter 9). Fisher was also responsible for a huge range of statistical tools, such as maximum likelihood estimation, as well as the understanding of a range of sampling distributions. Like Galton and Pearson, Fisher was also a Eugenicist, being Chairman of the University of Cambridge Eugenics Society. Indeed, only recently did Gonville and Caius College remove a stained-glass window commemorating him due to these beliefs.

The Reverand Thomas Bayes (1701–1761)

Bayes was a Presbyterian minister who developed a specific statistical theorem "Bayes' theorem". This is a different field of statistics from that of Fisher and Pearson, and we will not be covering it later on in this book. To explain, statistics can be split into two camps, Frequentist (which is what we do with null hypothesis significance testing which we cover in detail in Chapter 9), while the other is Bayesian. In Bayesian statistics knowledge about, for example, associations between two variables is updated based on observed data. It doesn't revolve around testing and rejecting hypotheses (the probability of obtaining another data set with associations at least as extreme as that of those in a current data set), but rather tests the strength of evidence for a hypothesis using "Bayes factors". In quantitative methods in psychology, Bayesian statistics is much less common. Strangely enough, it is incredibly common for the naïve reader to interpret frequentist findings through a Bayesian lens, resulting in them making erroneous conclusions. It has been argued over the years that people are naturally Bayesian as people instinctively apply its form of reasoning.

Conclusion

Quantitative methods in psychology are a relatively young area of scientific research. Hopefully, you can now see how it developed from some key areas, with its feet planted in Psychophysics and intelligence testing. Some of the people key to its development held some deeply unpleasant beliefs but they are still influential on the field. It is of particular interest how the study of psychological processes demanded the development of new statistical tools, like Chi-squared tests and correlations, demonstrating how psychological enquiry and statistics go hand in hand.

Further Reading

Carpenter, S. K. (2005). Some neglected contributions of Wilhelm Wundt to the psychology of memory. *Psychological reports*, 97 (1), 63–73.
Khaleefa, O. (1999). Who is the founder of psychophysics and experimental psychology? *American journal of Islam and society*, 16 (2), 1–26.

References

Binet, A., & Simon, T. (1916). *The development of intelligence in children* (The Binet-Simon Scale). (E. S. Kite, Trans.). Williams & Wilkins Co. https://doi.org/10.1037/11069-000
Carpenter, S. K. (2005). Some neglected contributions of Wilhelm Wundt to the psychology of memory. *Psychological reports*, 97 (1), 63–73.
Cattell, J. M. (1890). Mental tests and measurements. *Mind*, 15, 373–380.
Curtis, M. E., & Glaser, R. (1981). Chapter 3: Changing Conceptions of Intelligence. *Review of research in education*, 9 (1), 111–148.
Fisher RA. 1956. *Statistical Methods and Scientific Inferences*. Oliver and Boyd, Edinburgh, UK.
Khaleefa, O. (1999). Who is the founder of psychophysics and experimental psychology?. *American journal of Islam and society*, 16 (2), 1–26.
Murre, J. M. J., Dros, J. (2015) Replication and analysis of Ebbinghaus' Forgetting Curve. *PLoS ONE* 10(7): e0120644. https://doi.org/10.1371/journal.pone.0120644
Pearson, K. (1930). *The Life, Letters and Labours of Francis Galton*, 3 vols. in 4 (Cambridge: Cambridge Univ. Press, 1914-1930), Vol. Illa, p. 248.
Steffens B. *Ibn al-Haytham: First Scientist*. Morgan Reynolds Publishing; Greensboro, NC: 2006.

Chapter 3

Understanding psychological phenomena through numbers – The scientific process

Introduction

This chapter will discuss psychology as a science and the general scientific process. It will then focus on hypothesis generation, taking you through the difference between "fuzzy" hypotheses (broad statements open to interpretation) and clear operationalised hypotheses. This will lead to describing independent and dependent variables using multiple examples from a range of fields in psychology. Common confusion with the concepts of dependent and independent variables will also be looked at.

Psychology as a science

In this book, we are discussing psychology as a quantitative science. This means that we must follow the scientific method. **In the simplest terms, the scientific method involves making a prediction (a hypothesis) and then conducting an experiment to test if the prediction is correct.** However, the scientific method involves quite a few steps, as outlined in Figure 3.1. If you want to understand the philosophical underpinning of the scientific method please read Box 3.1 on Karl Popper and Box 3.2 on Thomas Kuhn.

Working through the scientific process

Generate a hypothesis

A hypothesis is a prediction (or "bold conjecture" see Box 3.1) about what you think you will observe in your scientific study. This is based on theory and past

Hypothesis. A prediction about what you will observe in your scientific study.

DOI: 10.4324/9781032656564-4

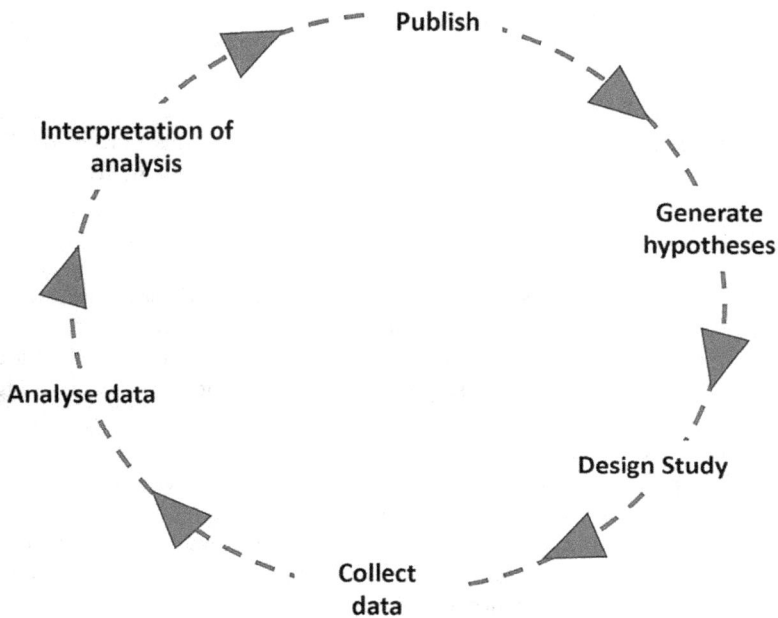

Figure 3.1 The scientific process

research. If you just have a vague idea e.g. "People with hazel eyes are all psychopaths", then although this is a hypothesis, it is not based on anything – you need a *reason* for a hypothesis. Indeed, the introduction of a research publication can be viewed as a great big justification for a hypothesis.

There are key things to understand about a hypothesis. Let's consider two hypotheses: **Professor Z (based on someone I used to work with, who proposed this type of stuff):**

> *"Just as people are dying, they relive their entire lives, and we are unaware if our lives are real or the reliving of a life on the deathbed"* (apologies for any existential crises caused).

Professor X (not the X-Men one):

> *"Consuming six units of alcohol will significantly increase accidents in a driving simulator compared to when no units are consumed"*

Hypotheses must follow some basic criteria, let's look at these two hypotheses in terms of these criteria:

1 Hypotheses must be testable, Professor Z has produced an untestable hypothesis there is no practical way of doing this. Professor X's hypothesis is testable, it's easy to see how this experiment could be set up (more on this later).
2 Hypotheses predict relationships. Professor Z's hypothesis does not predict any relationships; it is merely a statement that something occurs, with a second clause that doesn't explore any variables. Professor X predicts a relationship between units consumed and errors.
3 Hypotheses must be concise. Professor Z rambles and includes speculation. Professor X states simple relationships with no waffling.
4 Hypotheses must not be ambiguous. Prof Z is ambiguous, what is being measured? How is it being measured? What qualifies as reliving their entire lives? This is vague! Prof X has no ambiguity, the outcome is clear as is the manipulation (6 units vs. no units).
5 Hypotheses must be based on theory/past research. We don't know for sure without reading up, but believe me, Prof Z's hypothesis is just wild speculation and not based on anything (particularly the second clause which reads like the plot to the *Matrix*). Prof X's is based on a large amount of research into the effects of alcohol on cognitive functioning

When producing hypotheses or reading others' hypotheses keep these criteria in mind. There is another factor to consider, which I think is particularly important, this is to *operationalise* your hypotheses. This means that you want to talk about variables in the terms in which you will measure them. Of course, this cannot be done until you design your study so we will consider that first.

Design Study

Designing a study is a huge part of what we talk about in this book and cannot be simply summarised here. When I talk about designing a study, I am referring to a lot of things:

• Selecting independent and dependent variables (This chapter and Chapters 4, 13, 14).
• Selecting how you are going to measure and explore these relationships through different study designs (within-subjects, between subjects, correlational; Chapters 5, 6, 7).

- Choosing your sample of interest (Chapter 8), the size of your sample (Chapter 9), and the strategy for recruiting your sample (Chapter 10).

You need to think about all these things very carefully before you set about collecting data. If you don't, you may create a study that fails to test what you intended or one where the findings apply to a small group. As an applied statistician, if I had a pound for every time someone has come to be with a data set that cannot test their hypothesis, I'd be rich (well, I'd have an extra £39, but you get my point). Good design maximises the chances of you producing quality knowledge (note I don't say success, thinking in terms of "*success*" leads to bad things – see Chapter 15).

Collect data

Collecting data involves you sticking to your design! However, there are some considerations when it comes to collecting data. One is practicality, how are you going to do it, in a lab? Online? Different methods have different advantages and disadvantages. Also, when collecting data you need to think about what you will do when things go wrong! What likely obstacles are there going to be, and what could mitigate them? This part is very much common sense!

Analyse data

The fun part! (maybe that's just me). Once you have your data you need to analyse it effectively. The broad theory of data analysis is covered in Chapter 9 and specific methods are covered in Chapters 11 and 12. As well as formal data analysis you will also want to visualise your data effectively.

Interpretation of the analysis

Firstly, you will need to know if you have supported your hypothesis or not. Remember what makes a good hypothesis; if your hypothesis is unclear then you may not be able to explicitly say if you have supported it or not! Next, you will also need to understand your results in terms of past research – is it consistent with it? If not, why not? Perhaps it's due to limitations of the method, a different sample than past research, or maybe the theory tested us wrong (and we are now in "revolutionary science" – see box 3.1). However, you must understand what your data can and can't tell you – this is covered in detail throughout Section 4 of this book.

Publish

The (in my opinion) most frustrating part. You want to share your results with others. This means you need to publish them in a scientific journal. There are thousands of journals to choose from. You submit your research and then you have to go through peer review in which "experts" review the paper and give comments on it, stating if it should be accepted, revised according to their comments and accepted, or should be rejected. Often this process is really valuable and helps improve a paper, sometimes it is deeply frustrating and makes you want to quit academia and opt for the dog walking career that you would love. We will look into some of the issues with publishing in Chapters 15 and 16.

Operationalising hypotheses: Avoiding "fuzzy" hypotheses

You will recall that I previously discussed how a good hypothesis is **operationalised, i.e. the prediction that you make is stated in terms of how the variables considered are being measured.** Let's look at our example of a good hypothesis again:

> **Operationalised.** When predictions are stated in terms of how the variables considered are being measured.

"Consuming six units of alcohol will significantly increase accidents in a driving simulator, compared to when no units are consumed".

In this case, how we are measuring our variables is clearly stated. It is clear that we are measuring the number of accidents in a driving simulator. We did not say:

"Consuming six units of alcohol will make driving significantly worse, compared to when no units are consumed".

This is unclear, it could mean the number of accidents, the number of times someone drifts out of lane, fails to use indicators, ignores road signs etc. I would call this a "fuzzy" hypothesis. This sort of non-specific hypothesis can lead to unscrupulous research practices (see Chapter 15), as a dishonest researcher could test all these ways of measuring "worse driving" in the hope of supporting the hypothesis.

With our first example, the reader knows that to support the hypothesis we need to see differences in the number of accidents, not anything else. Furthermore, the researcher has also made it clear that there are two conditions in this experiment, (1) consuming six units of alcohol and (2) consuming no units of alcohol. The reader knows what the experimenter is manipulating in this experiment. Again, if this part of the hypothesis was written badly, it would make it "fuzzy"

"Alcohol consumption will increase accidents in a driving simulator".

Here, we have our operationalised measure of poor driving, but now the alcohol consumption part is unclear. What does alcohol consumption mean in this context, one unit? Thirty units? What is the effect of alcohol being compared to? You can't just give people alcohol and observe the number of accidents in a driving simulator; you don't know if they would have had accidents if they did not consume alcohol.

It is through this process of operationalising our variables that we understand psychological phenomena through numbers. We take the idea of "Alcohol use" and operationalise that as two conditions (six units consumed, no units consumed) and another concept "driving performance" and change that into a number (number of accidents in the driving simulator). So, we have taken broad concepts and turned these into numbers which we can then analyse to test our hypothesis.

Operationalising hypotheses: Independent variables and dependent variables

Hopefully, now you understand what makes a clear hypothesis. However, when we think about hypotheses we should think about them in terms of independent and dependent variables. This will also help you understand the analysis that you will need to do.

Independent variables (IVs)

An independent variable is a variable that is *independent* of the thing you are trying to observe changes/differences in. In experimental research, it can be the thing that you are manipulating to cause a change in an outcome. So in our hypothesis,

*"**Consuming six units of alcohol** will significantly increase accidents in a driving simulator, compared to when **no units are consumed**"*.

Independent variable (IV). A variable that is independent of the thing you are trying to observe changes/differences in. In experimental research, it can be the thing that you are manipulating to cause a change in an outcome.

The independent variable is the bit in bold, as we are giving people six units of alcohol OR no units of alcohol. The researcher is in charge of that bit of the experiment and is directly manipulating it themselves. It is not influenced by anything else in the experiment, particularly the outcome (number of errors).

Dependent variables (DVs)

A dependent variable *depends* on the influence of the IV, it is what we expect to change as a result of the effect of the independent variable. It can be seen as our outcome of interest.

"Consuming six units of alcohol will significantly increase <u>accidents</u> <u>in a driving simulator</u>, compared to when no units are consumed".

> **Dependent variable (DV).** A variable that depends on the influence of the IV, it is what we expect to change as a result of the effect of the independent variable. It can be seen as our outcome of interest.

In our example, the dependent variable is the part that is underlined, we are seeing if the amount of accidents we record participants having in our simulator is *dependent* upon whether alcohol is consumed or not.

It is important that you familiarize yourself with these two terms, they will come up a lot in your degree. Not only will they help you clearly understand the research that you do but also help you understand others' research.

Here are some other examples of hypotheses with the independent variable in bold and the dependent variable that's underlined:

1   **"People listening to discordant music will take longer than those listening to calming music** to complete a <u>mental arithmetic puzzle</u>".
2   **"Students who read the BPS introduction to quantitative methods** book will have higher <u>final degree marks</u> than those who **do not read it".**
3   **"Children exposed to fast food advertising in a lab** will consume <u>more calories</u> than those **not exposed to fast food advertising".**
4   **"Participants who consumed drugs in adolescence** will have poorer <u>working memory</u> in adulthood than **participants who did not".**
5   **"Higher scores on an impulsivity questionnaire** (Barrett impulsivity scales) will predict <u>increased risky sexual behaviour</u>".

Independent variables (IVs): A common confusion

Earlier on I said that an independent variable is a variable that is independent of the thing you are trying to observe changes/differences in.

Now in hypothesis 2, we have a problem; maybe more diligent students are more likely to read this book (pat yourself on the back), and would have done better anyway. So, we don't know that the independent variable of reading this book is fully independent of grades (a third factor – diligence may drive reading this book *and* grades). What we cannot be certain of here is a causal relationship. This problem is also apparent in hypothesis 4 – maybe those with poorer working memory are more likely to consume drugs in adolescence. So, these variables may not be "independent" variables as you cannot be sure of the independence of them. However, people would still be likely to call them an independent variable when describing a study, and with the way I have worded the hypothesis it is clear I am predicting the IVs are going to influence the DVs. Notably, hypothesis 5 may also have this kind of problem, although it is less likely that risky sexual behaviour leads to impulsivity! In such a scenario, people often use the terms "predictor" and "outcome" instead of IV and DV respectively. Indeed, it can be argued that you should only use the term IV when you are certain the variable is truly independent. I believe this to be the case, however many people don't, and the point of this book is to get you ready for the harsh reality of quantitative methods!

So, to summarise, it is notable that the strict definition of an IV is a variable that is independent of the thing you are trying to observe, but people often use it even when this independence is not certain! It is often used to say it is the variable I will use to predict another variable.

No IVs or DVs?

In addition, we may have a hypothesis in which we don't think there is any IV or DV but rather two things that are associated with each other. If I bought into the early ideas of measuring intelligence, I may predict:

"There will be an association between reaction time and IQ".

In this case, I am predicting that the two things are associated with each other not one thing causes change in another. In this situation, I am not talking about any sort of direction so nothing can be remotely viewed as an IV and DV in this circumstance. This is often the case in correlational research.

If you are struggling with this, don't worry, I will cover different designs in detail (and will come back to hypotheses when I do so) in Chapters 5, 6 and 7.

Conclusion

The scientific method allows us to conduct quantitative research in a formulaic manner. This enables science to progress in an organised and robust manner. Each step has some core considerations that we will delve into in subsequent chapters. The key thing that we need to remember from this chapter is that we need clarity. Indeed, clarity at all stages is essential in quantitative methods. We want things to be clearly stated and not open to different interpretations. Only by making clear, operationalised hypotheses that are grounded in theory and past research are we able to study psychological processes and be confident in our results. In the next chapter, we are going to move on to discuss the types of numerical data we encounter and their properties.

Further Reading

Nola, R., & Sankey, H. (2014). Theories of scientific method: an introduction. Routledge.

Box 3.1 Karl Popper: Conjectures and refutations

The philosopher Karl Popper developed a model on how to conduct science. This was based on the argument that science is deductive rather than inductive.

Inductive: Data collected and then we use this data to produce theory/ generalisations. This can be problematic, for example, what if you collected a data set full of very atypical people and used that to base ideas about everyone on?

I go around 20 parks and observe the colour of the swans. I find all the swans are white. The inductive reasoning for this is that all swans are white.

Deductive: The researcher makes very specific predictions about relationships between variables (based on their knowledge). This prediction is then tested (i.e. data is collected). If the prediction is supported, then it is consistent with the knowledge you based it on. If it is supported (and the prediction was tested in a rigorous manner), the theory underlying the prediction is challenged or at perhaps the theory only works under certain conditions.

Popper would argue it doesn't matter how many white swans you observe you cannot prove your theory with this but finding a black swan shows your theory is wrong.

"... It is not the accumulation of observations which I have in mind when I speak of the growth of scientific knowledge, but the repeated overthrow of scientific theories and their replacement by better or more satisfactory ones."

"(Popper, 1963, p. 215)

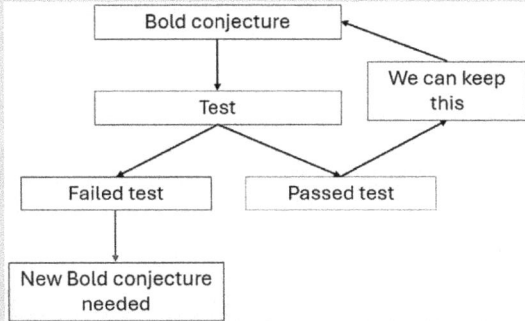

Box 3.2 Thomas Kuhn: Revolution!

Science works through a series of clear steps.

- Pre-science, where there is no clear paradigm being studied "ideas are still in their early stages and have not yet been subjected to rigorous scrutiny" (Kuhn, 1962, p. 9). Essentially things are being observed but there is not a clear theory accounting for it.
- Normal science, is where observations are put into a theoretical structure. This makes the science well-organised, and researchers are testing all aspects of a theory.
- Revolutionary Science: The observations that are not consistent with theory start to mount up.
- New paradigm that explains the inconsistencies

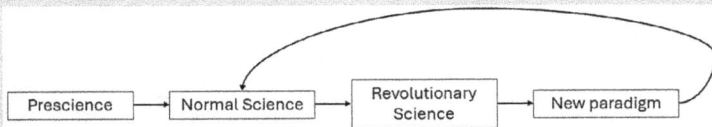

References

Kuhn, Thomas S. (1970). *The structure of scientific revolutions.* 2nd ed. Chicago: University of Chicago Press

Popper, K. R. (1963). Science as falsification. *Conjectures and refutations.* 1, 33–39.

Chapter 4

The types of numerical data we encounter and their properties

Introduction

In this chapter, we will discuss different forms of quantitative data (known as nominal, ordinal, scale and ratio) and the properties of each. I will also demonstrate how it is often possible to measure an outcome using different methods. Then we will move on to consider the suitability of different forms of data and the consequences of choosing different measures. The appropriate way to numerically describe different types of data will then be examined.

Data types

There are three core types of quantitative data that we encounter, however, within these, there are sub-types as well. Let's explore these data types:

Nominal data (also called categorical or discrete data)

Nominal data is simply when we have different categories of things. For example, I collect data from ten people about the first pet that they owned:

> **Nominal data.** this is purely categorical data, where categories can't be put in a logical order.

Table 4.1 Nominal data

Participant	Pet
1	Dog
2	Cat
3	None
4	Fish
5	Cat
6	Dog

DOI: 10.4324/9781032656564-5

Participant	Pet
7	Dog
8	None
9	None
10	None

This, although consisting of "words" is quantitative data, indeed we could easily change these words into numbers.

Table 4.2 Nominal data converted into numbers

Participant	Pet	Pet (code)
1	Dog	1
2	Cat	2
3	None	0
4	Fish	3
5	Cat	2
6	Dog	1
7	Dog	1
8	None	0
9	None	0
10	None	0

This is commonly done, but it is important to understand that these numbers have absolutely no meaning in themselves other than being a label. This is the key thing about nominal data – the categories cannot be put in any logical order. In the above example, None is coded as 0, Dog is coded as 1, cat is coded as 2 and Fish is coded as 3. These numerical labels are *arbitrary*. There is no reason why the data couldn't be labelled as:

Table 4.3 Nominal data converted into numbers using a different coding system

Participant	Pet	Pet (code)
1	Dog	2
2	Cat	1
3	None	3
4	Fish	0
5	Cat	1
6	Dog	2
7	Dog	2
8	None	3

Participant	Pet	Pet (code)
9	None	3
10	None	3

This is an equally valid way to do it. The arbitrary nature of nominal data means there are limited things that you can do with it mathematically. You cannot order it unless you base it on your opinion. For example, I would order it as Dog > Fish > None > cat (I have a dog and am allergic to cats but this is my personal judgement), I'm sure that you may put this in a different order. However, putting things in order based on your opinions is not very scientific! Due to this, we have to be very careful about how we describe nominal data, which we will discuss in the next section.

There are lots of things that we measure that produce nominal data. Let's look at another example; here we ask participants if they ever drink alcohol or not:

Table 4.4   Another example of nominal data converted into numbers

Participant	Ever Drink	Ever Drink (code)		Participant	Ever Drink (code)
1	No	0		1	0
2	Yes	1		2	1
3	Yes	1		3	1
4	Yes	1	Often, your	4	1
5	Yes	1	data would →	5	1
6	Yes	1	look like this	6	1
7	No	0		7	0
8	Yes	1		8	1
9	Yes	1		9	1
10	No	0		10	0

So, our participants are categorised as non-drinkers (0), or drinkers (1). Again, these are discrete groups; you cannot be in both, you either drink alcohol or not.

Other examples of nominal data include:

Hair colour – Red, brown, blonde, black, grey, white etc
Nationality – British, American, Spanish, Kenyan etc
Favourite type of music – Country (this is the best), Rock, Jazz, Hip-hop etc

Now I know some of you may say what if someone has black hair with bits of white in it, what if they dye their hair? Or is a dual-national; these are not discrete groups! Yes, this is true, but as the person asking the questions, you make the rules!

So, when asking the question about nationality you could state "If you are dual nationality then please state the country you identify with the most". Or, instead, you could have a response that is dual nationality.

Likewise, for hair colour, you could say, "If you dye your hair please state your natural colour". Essentially, you need to consider how to measure the outcome and think about what options you will need.

Ordinal data (ranked data)

Ordinal data is when we have different categories but they can be put in a clear order. Remember, with nominal data like pet type we can't put them in a clear order as categories are arbitrary. With ordinal data, we can do this. For example, imagine I collect data on the level of education.

> **Ordinal data.** Categorical data but the categories can be put in a logical ascending/descending order.

Table 4.5 Ordinal data

Participant	Education
1	GCSE
2	Undergraduate
3	A-level
4	A-level
5	Postgraduate
6	GCSE
7	A-Level
8	Undergraduate
9	A-level
10	Undergraduate

As before, I could give these a numerical label, indeed with ordinal data we would want to do this so we can analyse it effectively:

Table 4.6 Ordinal data coded

Participant	Education	Education (code)		Participant	Education (code)
1	GCSE	1		1	1
2	Undergraduate	3		2	3
3	A-level	2	Usually, your data would look like this	3	2
4	A-level	2		4	2
5	Postgraduate	4		5	4
6	GCSE	1		6	1
7	A-Level	2		7	2
8	Undergraduate	3		8	3
9	A-level	2		9	2
10	Undergraduate	3		10	3

The numbers I have given to the different education levels are really important. In nominal data it doesn't matter how I label things, in ordinal data the numbers relate to rank order.

- Rank 1 – GCSE
- Rank 2 – A-Level
- Rank 3 – Undergraduate
- Rank 4 – Postgraduate

I have ordered them from the lowest level of qualification to the highest, and then given them a number. Technically, I could number them from the highest being rank 1, and the lowest being rank 4, and this would only affect the "direction" of relationships (I cover this in Chapter 7). The key point is that I can objectively rank them in order. This is why ordinal and nominal data differ. One thing to note is that the numbers we give the different categories do not have a true mathematical relationship with each other: you can't multiply GCSEs by two to get an A-Level (1 x 2=2), and you can't multiply A-levels by two and get a Postgraduate (2x2=4) – that's just nonsensical!

Another good example is data derived from Likert scales (pronounced Lick-Ert NOT Like-Ert). These are when we give response options like this:

Statement: Coldplay are a terrible band

- Strongly Disagree (1)
- Disagree (2)
- Agree (3)
- Strongly agree (4)

Again, we can order responses but there's no real mathematical relationship between the numbers. Furthermore, we can't quantify the strength of feeling within these categories. In response to this question, I would "Strongly Agree". You may also strongly agree, but I can guarantee that you don't feel as strongly as I do about it (I have, after all, worked my hatred of Coldplay into a textbook).

However, it is notable that while an individual Likert response is ordinal, if you have a validated questionnaire (see Chapter 14 for what I mean by validation) that asks multiple questions to give a total score or an average score then this would not be ordinal data. This is a really common mistake! This data would be interval data which I discuss next.

Interval and Ratio data

Interval data (sometimes called continuous data although I think that is misleading), where we can order numbers and the numbers have an actual meaning. For example, we wish to measure body temperature after someone is put under extreme stress.

Interval data. Data where we can order numbers and the numbers are measured on a scale with equal intervals.

Table 4.7 Interval/ratio data

Participant	Body temp (Degrees Celsius)
1	37.2
2	36.8
3	38.2
4	36.4
5	38.9
6	36.5
7	37.7
8	38.3
9	37.4
10	38.2

These numbers have a true mathematical relationship with each other; for example, we know that participant 1 (37.2 degrees) is exactly one degree lower than participants 3 and 10. So for interval data, we have a quantifiable understanding of the difference between numbers. We don't have that with nominal or ratio data. One thing to note with interval data is that the 0 is arbitrary. For example, temperature in degrees Celsius has a 0 (and minus values too) but that 0 is not "absence of temperature", it is just a temperature of a certain level (freezing point of water).

Ratio data **has these same properties as interval data plus an absolute zero.** The number of goals scored by a football team in a season would be ratio. They cannot score less than zero goals. It may be the case that you could score something as interval or ratio. For example, temperature measured in degrees Celsius can have a minus, however, temperature measured in Kelvin cannot go

Ratio data. Data where we can order numbers and the numbers are measured on a scale with equal intervals and there is an absolute zero.

below zero ("absolute zero"). Ratio data is very common: scores on a test, reaction time, age, weight etc are all ratio data.

Notably, the ratio and interval distinction is not particularly consequential, it's just ratio has zero as a reference point. When doing some more advanced things such as data transformation and other mathematical operations on variables having minus figures can produce some challenges but we don't need to be concerned about that in this book.

Same thing, different measures

We can measure the same thing using different methods and produce different data types, particularly ordinal vs. interval/ratio. Let's say we are running a study looking at personality traits that predict an individual's body mass index (BMI). BMI is used to judge if someone is underweight, normal weight, overweight or obese.

Table 4.8 Coding the same data in different ways

Participant	BMI	BMI category	BMI category (num)
1	22	Normal weight	3
2	38	Obese	5
3	27	Overweight	4
4	21	Normal weight	3
5	16	Severely underweight	1
6	30	Obese	5
7	26	Overweight	4
8	29	Overweight	4
9	42	Obese	5
10	18	Underweight	2

Severely underweight – BMI less than 16.5, Underweight – BMI under 18.5 kg, Normal weight – BMI greater than or equal to 18.5 to 24.9, Overweight – BMI greater than or equal to 25 to 29.9, Obesity – BMI greater than or equal to 30

You can see in this example that we have participants' raw BMI (ratio) and have put them into categories (ordinal). This means that we can have the same data but express it with different data types. Which should you use in such circumstances? As a general rule, I would use the interval/ratio version rather than the ordinal one. The interval data contains more information than the data put into the groups, meaning it has more sensitivity. To look at specific issues around this sensitivity, we will look at participants 6, 8, and 9:

Table 4.9 Problems with recoding data into categories

Participant	BMI	BMI category	BMI category (num)
6	30	Obese	5
8	29	Overweight	4
9	42	Obese	5

Participant **6** is in the Obese category, as is participant **9**. When we look at the BMI column these two participants have very different BMIs (the difference between them being 12).

Participant **6** (in the obese category) is in a different category than participant **8** who is in the overweight category; when we look at the BMI column these two participants have an almost identical BMI, with the difference being 1.

The ordinal data treats participants 6 and 9 as having the same BMI (when we know they are very different). Participants 6 and 8 are very similar to each other but the ordinal data puts them in different categories. As a general rule, you are much better off keeping as much information as possible with your data, so the interval measure here is better than the ordinal measure. I often see students measuring age with ordinal categories (18–24, 25–30 etc); just taking their age in years is always preferable!

How do you pick how you will measure variables?

When designing quantitative studies, you will need to decide how to measure variables. Sometimes this will be forced upon you. For example, if I am interested in whether someone quits smoking or not then you have a categorical outcome of quitting smoking or not quitting smoking (of course how you define quitting smoking is also important e.g., complete abstinence vs. less than X number of cigarettes smoked). In some situations, you have to decide on how to measure something. For example, let's look at university performance:

Table 4.10 Another example of the same data coded in different ways

Participant	Pass or Fail	Categorical grade	Final average
1	P	1	80
2	P	2.1	68
3	P	3	45
4	F	F	28
5	P	2.2	52
6	P	2.1	65

We can look at this through a nominal, ordinal or ratio lens. In this (and most cases) you will be better off measuring the variable with the most granularity, so the ratio (final average) is the most useful. However, this depends on the research question; maybe you are only interested if, for example, socioeconomic status predicts passing a university degree. In that case, you only really need the data at the nominal level (Pass or Fail) as that is what you are testing.

When thinking about how to measure variables of interest, it is always a good idea to see how other researchers have done it in the past. This will enable you to compare your results to others' more effectively, making it easier to discuss your findings. However, it should be noted that sometimes people measure things in sub-optimal manners, e.g. ordinal outcomes when there is a more effective interval measure.

Now there are often practical considerations to take into account. If you are doing secondary data analysis, where you analyse a pre-existing data set, then you will be limited by how the data was collected. Furthermore, it is sometimes hard to measure things optimally and get an accurate response. For example, I may wish to measure your social media use. If I asked you how many minutes per week you spend using social media, how accurate do you think that you would be?

Sometimes how you measure something depends on what you want to be able to say. For example, I may be interested to know if antidepressant tablets are effective. I do some research and end up with two options for measuring depression.

1   Using the depression scale from the Depression, Anxiety, and Stress Scale (DASS). This will give me a ratio measure of depression, with higher scores meaning more depressed
2   Using whether the participants have a clinical diagnosis of depression, this gives me a nominal outcome of being diagnosed with depression or not diagnosed with depression

Which should I pick?

There's no right or wrong answer here, but there are things you should consider. If I want to be able to say that antidepressant tablets "cure" depression I will need to use the clinical diagnosis as this will tell me whether the tablets prevent people from having the disorder. If I were to use the questionnaire outcome, antidepressants may reduce scores on the scale but the participants may still all have clinical levels of depression i.e. the decrease did not take their symptoms to a sub-clinical level. However, if I am interested in whether antidepressants reduce the amount of depression symptoms or the severity of depression, then the DASS scale may well be sufficient for my needs.

Describing different types of data

These different types of data (nominal, ordinal, and interval/ratio) need to be described in different ways. When doing quantitative research we almost always produce what we call descriptive statistics. These give our reader an understanding of our data in terms of two things: Central tendency and Spread.

Central tendency

This is a way of describing the centre point in the data set, which has quite different meanings depending on the type of data.

Mode

The mode is the most common response; this is most useful for nominal data. Let's look at the pet ownership example again.

Mode. The most common value.

Table 4.11 The mode of a data set

Participant	Pet	Pet (code)
1	Dog	1
2	Cat	2
3	**None**	0
4	Fish	3
5	Cat	2
6	Dog	1
7	Dog	1
8	**None**	0
9	**None**	0
10	**None**	0

The modal (most common) response in the data is "None". There are four cases of this, (three for dog, two for cat and one for fish). If you were to write down these responses on 10 different pieces of paper and put them in a bag and then draw one at random and guess what it will be, then your best guess would be "None" as it's the most common response. The mode can also be useful for ordinal data. However, it tends to be less useful for interval/ratio data. In our body temperature example, no two people may have the same temperature so there is no mode, and if by chance two people did then that's not telling me about the central tendency of the data.

Median

The median is the middle response; it is very useful for ordinal data, although it can also be reported for interval/ratio data. Let's look at the education-level data to explore medians.

> **Median.** The middle value.

Table 4.12 The median of a variable (even number of values)

Row	Participant	Education
1	1	1
2	6	1
3	3	2
4	4	2
5	7	2
6	9	2
7	2	3
8	8	3
9	10	3

> We order the data from lowest (GCSE) to highest (postgraduate)

Once the data has been ordered, the median is the middle value. If we have an even number of responses then there is no single middle value, rows 5 and 6 are the two middle values (there are four numbers before 5 and four numbers after 6). So, we have two median values, although in this case, both values are **2** (A-level), so in our data the median level of education is **2** (A-level).

If we have an odd number of rows then we would have a single median value, so in the below we have nine participants, meaning the middle value is 5 (there are four numbers before 5, and four numbers after 5). So, our median is just the very central value, and it's 2 again.

Table 4.13 The median of a variable (odd number of values)

Participant	Education
1	1
2	3
3	2
4	2
5	4
6	1
7	2
8	3
9	2
10	3

Row	Participant	Education
1	1	1
2	6	1
3	3	2
→ 4	4	2
5	7	2
6	9	2
7	2	3
8	8	3
9	10	3
10	5	4

What if the numbers are even and there are two different middle values? Let's say our data looked like the below, and we have two central values (5 and 6) but these have two different ordinal values, 2 and 3.

Table 4.14 The median of a variable (even number of values, with different values at the midpoint)

Row	Participant	Education
1	1	1
2	6	1
3	3	2
4	4	2
5	7	2
6	9	3
7	2	3
8	8	3
9	10	3
10	5	4

In this case, the median is:

$$\frac{2+3}{2} = 2.5$$

Mean

The average response. This is most useful for interval/ratio data although it is common with ordinal data as well. I am sure you are all familiar with average responses; it is the sum

Mean. The average value.

of all the responses (i.e. add up all the scores) divided by the number of responses. Let's look at our body temperature data again.

Table 4.15 Interval data with the sum included

Participant	Body temp (Degrees Celsius)
1	37.2
2	36.8
3	38.2
4	36.4
5	38.9

Participant	Body temp (Degrees Celsius)
6	36.5
7	37.7
8	38.3
9	37.4
10	38.2
Sum	375.6

The sum is 375.6 then we divide this by 10 and get 37.56 as our mean body temperature. If I had to guess the body temperature of these ten participants, I would guess 37.56 for them all; this would be the most accurate way to guess (without relying on dumb luck!). In some situations, the mean can be misleading; for example in a small data set with a few extreme scores. For example, here I had seven students do an incredibly hard quantitative test but one student has memorised this book so is well prepared:

Table 4.16 The effect of extreme values in small data sets

Student	Test score (/100)
1	8
2	15
3	16
4	19
5	20
6	21
7	100
Sum	194

This gives us a mean score of 27.7 (194/7) but all barring one student scored a fair bit below this value so it is not really a good measure of central tendency when describing my data. The median in this example is 19 which is a better representation of the overall samples' central tenancy.

It is also worth noting that the mean has absolutely no value when it comes to nominal data! People often code nominal data as numbers. I cannot tell you the number of times I have seen students code Sex as 0 (male) 1 (female) and then say the mean sex for the sample was .87 (or something) that doesn't make sense! Similarly, here is the pet data:

Table 4.17a The nominal pet data – two examples of a common mistake

Participant	Pet	Pet (code)
1	Dog	1
2	Cat	2
3	None	0
4	Fish	3
5	Cat	2
6	Dog	1
7	Dog	1
8	None	0
9	None	0
10	None	0

The sum of the pet (code) column is 10 so I would say the average response is a dog (10/10=1) (when it's not the most common – "None" is).

Table 4.17b The nominal pet data – two examples of a common mistake

Participant	Pet (code)
1	1
2	2
3	0
4	3
5	2
6	1
7	1
8	3
9	0

Furthermore, the average response is 1.44 which would mean that the average response is 1.44 (a cat-dog hybrid?). Moreover, the numbers I assigned to groups are arbitrary I could have none as 3 and dog as 0 this would change the mean!

Spread of data

The spread of data is really important too. Knowing the central tendency gives one piece of the puzzle but we also need to understand how spread out scores are. There are several different ways to do this, and which one is appropriate is dependent upon the type of data.

First of all, for nominal data there is no real measure of spread, you can just state the number in each category (frequency distribution). But for ordinal and interval/ratio data there are several measures we can use.

Range

The range is simply the difference between the highest and lowest score e.g.

In the body temperature data, the lowest temperature is 36.4 and the highest is 38.9 giving a range of 2.5 (38.9–36.4).

In our test score data, the range is 92 (100–8)

> **Range.** The spread of values from the minimum value to the maximum value.

> **Interquartile range.** The spread of values within the middle 50% of data (ignoring the top and bottom 25%).

Table 4.18 The ratio/interval data – body temperature

Participant	Body temp (Degrees Celsius)
1	37.2
2	36.8
3	38.2
4	36.4
5	38.9
6	36.5
7	37.7
8	38.3
9	37.4
10	38.2

Sometimes we report the **interquartile range instead. This is the range of the middle 50% of data**. Let's look at an expanded version of our test score data:

Table 4.19 The ratio/interval data – with the interquartile range shown

Student	Test score (/100)
1	8
2	10
3	11
4	12
5	16
6	19
7	20
8	21
9	22
10	22
11	24
12	100

Ignore the top and bottom 25%

We remove the top and bottom 25% of the data and then work out the range of the remaining data, in this case *22–12* = 10. This is often done when there are some very extreme values influencing the range. In this example, the range is 92 and the interquartile range is 10.

Variance:

The variance is the average of the squared differences between each value and the mean. Yes, I know that sounds confusing so let's take a look at using the test score data. You will recall that the mean

> **Variance.** The average of the squared differences between each value and the mean.

from this data is 27.7, so we subtract the mean from each value (e.g. row one is 8–27.7 = -19.7). Then we square this difference.

We now have the **Sum of Squares.** To turn this into the variance we divided it by N (if it's a population we are looking at) or N-1 if it's a sample (we have a sample, more on this in Chapter 8).

$$So\ our\ variance\ is: \frac{6093.43}{7-1} = \frac{6093.43}{6} = 1015.57$$

The full formula for the variance which we have just done is below (it looks scarier than it is).

$$\sigma^2 = \frac{\Sigma(X - \bar{X})^2}{n-1}$$

x = a value, $\bar{x}$ = the mean, Σ = sum of, n= the sample size

The variance is an incredibly important statistic, particularly when we are testing hypotheses (which we discuss in Chapter 9). However, it is not that helpful as a descriptive statistic, so you are unlikely to see it reported. Instead, we report the standard deviation.

Table 4.20 The ratio/interval data for test score – calculating the variance

Test score (/100)	Difference from the mean	Squared difference from the mean
8	-19.7	388.09
15	-12.7	161.29
16	-11.7	136.89
19	-8.7	75.69
20	-7.7	59.29
21	-6.7	44.89
100	72.3	5227.29
		Sum: **6093.43**

Standard deviation

The standard deviation is simply the square root of the variance, so its formula is:

$$SD = \sqrt{\frac{\Sigma(\mathbf{X} - \bar{\mathbf{X}})^2}{n-1}}$$

Standard deviation. the Square root of the variance.

So the SD for our test score is $\sqrt{1015.57}$ = 36.87. The standard deviation is another measure of dispersion around the mean. In this example, it is quite big but it is made bigger by the one person with the high score (100) compared to the sample mean (27.7) and our sample is tiny.

Let's expand the example. Let's say I have 1000 people complete the test and the average score is 65 and the standard deviation is 8. I can put this on a graph known as a histogram. This simply visualises how many people got each score on the exam. So, the Y axis (vertical one labelled Frequency) is the number of people who have each score.

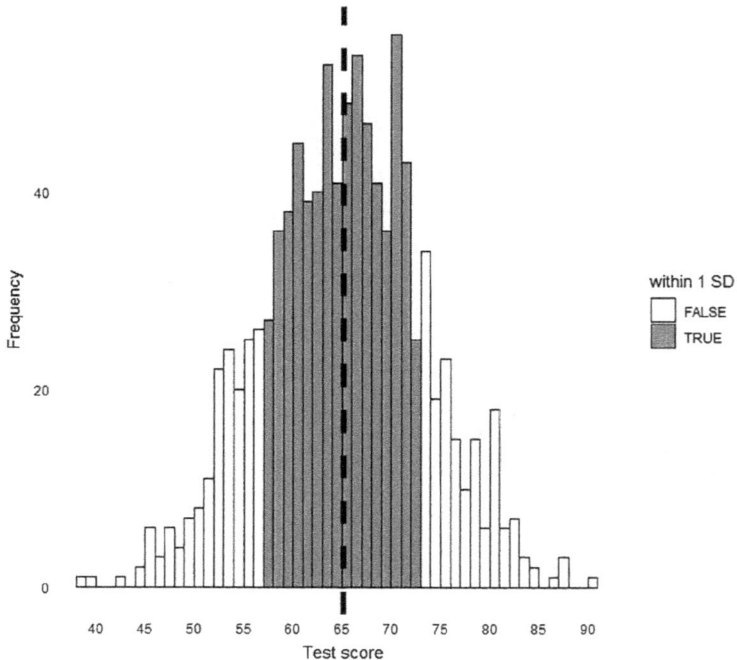

Figure 4.1 A histogram of test score data showing the mean and one standard deviation

The mean is represented by the dotted line. The standard deviation uses the mean as a reference point. I have plotted one standard deviation above, and below, the mean in grey. A score from 65 up to 73 is one standard deviation above the mean, and a score from 57 to 65 is one standard deviation below the mean. So, everyone in red is one standard deviation from the mean.

Critically, 68% of a sample will fall one standard deviation from the mean (so 680 participants will be in red, the remaining 320 are in white). 95% of participants fall within two standard deviations, and 99.7% fall within three standard deviations. Because of this property, the standard deviation is incredibly useful as a statistic. It is almost always reported with the mean. It can be reported with ordinal data if a mean is given with it, although there are limitations in its interpretation in this case. It has no value with nominal data though!

Conclusion

There are different types of data, each with its own properties. When choosing how to measure something, it is important to think about the consequences of the measurement type, what it will allow you to say about the data, and how sensitive any analysis will be. It is also important to remember that different data types are described in different ways and that some methods of describing data simply cannot be used with certain types of data; don't make this mistake! Below is a summary of how to describe different types of data, in red are the main methods for each type.

Table 4.21 A reminder for different types of data and how to describe them

Data type	Central tendency	Spread
Nominal	Mode	Frequency distribution
Ordinal	Median/mode (people do give means sometimes)	Range, interquartile range (sometimes you will see Standard deviations)
Interval/Ratio	Mean (can use median, mode is often not useful)	Standard deviation (range/ interquartile range can be given)

Further Reading

Cohen, L., Manion, L., & Morrison, K. (2017). Descriptive statistics. In *Research methods in education* (pp. 753–775). Routledge.

Fisher, M. J., & Marshall, A. P. (2009). Understanding descriptive statistics. *Australian critical care*, 22(2), 93–97.

Section 2

Key Theories: An overview of the key theories and models relevant to the topic

Section 2 will focus on the building blocks of designing and understanding quantitative studies. This will then be mapped onto sampling methods, before finally addressing the core statistical of statistical significance.

At the end of Section 2, you will:

2.1 Understand different experimental designs, their pros and cons and what can be done to mitigate the latter.

2.2 Develop knowledge of quasi-experimental designs including their necessity, and what we can extrapolate from them.

2.3 Understand correlational designs, and why they are an important aspect of quantitative methods even if they cannot show causal relationships.

2.4 Become familiar with sampling theory and understand the language used when describing samples.

2.5 Gain an understanding of the key statistical concepts of null hypothesis significance testing, effect sizes, and confidence intervals.

DOI: 10.4324/9781032656564-6

Chapter 5

Experimental models

Introduction

In this chapter, a range of experimental designs will be discussed. Initially, it will describe what a true experiment is, why we conduct experiments, what is necessary to show causal effects in an experimental paradigm and threats to it. Subsequently, it will describe basic concepts of between and within-subjects designs and in doing so describe the advantages and disadvantages of each as well as what a researcher can do to mitigate disadvantages. Following this, it will build up from these basic concepts into more complicated multifactorial designs, describing the concept of an interaction.

What is an experiment?

An experiment is a research method that is used to test a hypothesis under controlled conditions. An experiment gives us control over variables; this means that we can take into account things we think will influence our results and miti-

> **Experiment.** A research method used to test a hypothesis under controlled conditions

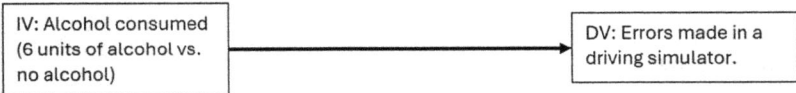

gate them. Doing this leads to more effective testing of our hypothesis. Ultimately, an experimental design aims to show a causal effect between an independent variable (IV) and the dependent variable (DV). A causal effect is where we can say (with as much confidence as possible) that the IV is the thing that is responsible for any change in the DV. Here's an example:

| IV: Alcohol consumed (6 units of alcohol vs. no alcohol) | → | DV: Errors made in a driving simulator. |

Figure 5.1 A simple experiment

DOI: 10.4324/9781032656564-7

We need to set up an experiment to ensure that the effect of alcohol on errors is causal. However, to do so we need to satisfy these three points:

> **Time order relationship.** Establishing the effect of one variable precedes another in time, indicating that the cause occurs before its effect.

- **An association between the two variables** – this is pretty obvious, there needs to be evidence that alcohol influences driving errors.
- **Time order relationship** – this is a fancy way of saying that **the IV variation must come before the DV variation**. So, our manipulation of the IV must cause the change in the DV, in an experimental paradigm this is quite straightforward, however as we will see in chapters 6 and 7 it is not easy in quasi-experiments or correlational research.
- **No alternative explanation aka non-spuriousness** – You need to ensure that **there is not something else that can account for an effect**. A simple example is that shark attacks are correlated with

> **Non-spuriousness key terms.** Establishing that there is not something else that can account for a relationship between two variables.

ice cream sales. Do ice creams attract sharks to beaches? Of course not! The alternative explanation is hot weather, when it's hot people swim in the sea and buy ice creams. When setting up an experiment you need to try and control for alternative explanations.

In Chapter 3 we talked about independent and dependent variables and it is in experimental designs where the independent variable is true to its definition:

> *"An independent variable is a variable that is independent of the thing you are trying to observe changes/differences in. In experimental research, it is **the thing that you are manipulating in order to cause a change in an outcome**."*

To show the time order relationship is straightforward as we are in charge of the manipulation - whether we give them alcohol or not! But we need to rule out other explanations. This is where we need to think about our design. There are two broad types of design we can use; within-subjects and between subjects. Each has its advantages and disadvantages, so we will explore setting up this experiment using both designs. Before we go into this, a brief comment on control groups

Control groups

One thing that experiments often have is a control group. If I am interested in the effect of alcohol on driving, I need to compare the effect of alcohol to something. I can't just give someone alcohol, observe them perform badly in a driving simulator, and say, "Yes alcohol makes you make more driving errors", this person may have

Control group. A condition where the experimental manipulation does not occur, used to compare the experimental condition(s) to.

made just as many if not more errors when not given alcohol, I wouldn't know. This is why you need a control condition. You need to carefully consider what a control condition is as it should be "equivalent". What I mean by this is that the two groups should be treated in the same way barring the specific bit of the intervention (e.g. in this case there is alcohol consumed). So my control group should consume something, but what they consume should not contain alcohol.

When we do studies that involve ingesting something that should have a physical/mental effect then we often have a placebo control group. This is where they have an expectation they are going to receive the substance but do not. This aims to rule out expected effects. For example, if people think they have consumed alcohol, they may feel the effects of alcohol because they expect to (this is a real phenomenon see, for example, Christiansen, Jennings, and Rose, 2016). So if we want to look at the pharmacological effects of alcohol (ignoring expectancies) we need to give people placebo alcohol (something they believe contains alcohol, tastes like alcohol but has no alcohol in it). This is why when testing different substances (e.g. anti-depressants) they are often done in placebo-controlled trials (for more detail see Gupta & Verma 2013).

Notably, equivalent control groups are important no matter the intervention; it could just be a task. For example, you may be interested in whether daily online cognitive behaviour therapy can reduce anxiety. You may be tempted to compare that to a control group who do nothing. This would not be equivalent, instead, you would compare them to a control group who do something online for the same duration as the cognitive behaviour therapy (with the only difference being there is no cognitive behaviour therapy component).

Between subject design (also called an independent groups/ samples/measures design)

In these designs, different participants are assigned to the different conditions of your independent variable. This means that one set of participants will be given 6 units of alcohol, and another different set will be given no alcohol.

Between subject design. A design where participants are assigned to (or are already in) different conditions (no participant is in more than one condition).

Alcohol group   **No alcohol group**

Figure 5.2 A between-subject design

Generally, we have an experimental group(s) and a control group when doing these designs. We observe whether the people in the alcohol (experimental) group make more errors than those we put in the no-alcohol group (control). This design has causality problems regarding alternative explanations.

The biggest problem is that individual differences may drive the effects rather than the independent variable. If the two groups are not balanced on some important variables, then this can mean that the effects are the product of this imbalance in participant characteristics and not the experimental manipulation.

For example, imagine I recruited participants for my alcohol group from first-year students and my non-alcohol group from third-year students. I may find that the alcohol group makes more errors so I support my hypothesis. However, there may be a third variable causing this effect – driving experience. It is likely that the sample of third-year students have more driving experience due to them being on average 2–3 years older than the alcohol group. So, we would not be able to rule out this causing the difference.

Many other individual differences may influence our results, maybe our alcohol group are all really heavy drinkers so are used to the effects of alcohol, this may reduce the number of errors that they make, producing no differences between our experimental conditions. This would lead to a possibly erroneous conclusion that we cannot support our hypothesis. What if we allowed self-selection into conditions? Heavy drinkers may be attracted by getting free alcohol whereas light drinkers or non-drinkers may be more likely to take part in the control condition; this means that groups would be imbalanced, and this again could influence our results.

Random assignment

Usually, we deal with this problem through random assignment to conditions. This means that different participant characteristics like age, drinking behaviour, and preexisting driving ability will be equally likely to be in each group (so these variables should be balanced across groups). This means that participant differences are unlikely to be causing the observed differences between conditions, and we can be confident that the IV is the cause of changes in the DV. Random assignment:

- Facilitates making causal inference
- Reduces individual differences between conditions
- Decreases the likelihood of having a false negative (e.g. concluding alcohol doesn't increase errors when in fact it does) and false positive (e.g. concluding alcohol does increase errors when in fact it doesn't)

Random assignment is a cornerstone of valid between-subjects designs. However, Other methods can be used.

Matched Groups

In a matched group design, you make sure that participants are matched on a range of characteristics that you believe will influence the DV, or how the IV influences the DV. So in our example, we could match on age, driving experience, weekly alcohol consumption, and so on. This method means that for every person in one condition, there is someone with the same characteristics in the other condition. This method is highly intuitive but often extremely impractical. It necessitates testing participants on a range of things before you do your experiment making it time-consuming and expensive. Random assignment is usually preferred.

Block randomisation

Sometimes researchers randomise in blocks, which is common in clinical trials. For example, in a trial into the effects of drinking artificially sweetened beverages on weight loss, I want to randomise participants into a sweetener or water condition. However, I may randomise them in blocks based on Sex (Male/Female) and whether they usually drink sweeteners (Yes/No). I did do this in a trial (see Harrold et al 2023). This is to be certain that we balance key characteristics across groups (so it is a bit like a crossover between random assignment and matching). What would block randomisation look like in the alcohol driving errors study? Imagine I have two blocks, sex (male/female) and whether they drive daily (Yes/No). I would make a spreadsheet like the one below to randomise participants (the spreadsheet would be much larger though!). The blocks have been colour-coded and the condition within each block has been randomised.

Sex	Regular driver	Condition
Female	Yes	Alcohol
Female	Yes	Control
Female	Yes	Control
Female	Yes	Alcohol
Female	No	Control
Female	No	Control
Female	No	Alcohol
Female	No	Alcohol
Male	Yes	Control
Male	Yes	Alcohol
Male	Yes	Control
Male	Yes	Alcohol
Male	No	Alcohol
Male	No	Control
Male	No	Control
Male	No	Alcohol

A participant would be recruited then we would ask their sex and whether they are a regular driver.

Our first participant is female, Non-regular driver so is in the control condition

Our second participant is male, regular driver so is in the control condition too

Our third participant is male, regular driver too, so is in the alcohol condition

We keep going with this and randomise all our participants, it doesn't matter if there isn't an even number of males and females or regular and non-regular drivers, we just ensure they are balanced across groups.

Figure 5.3 How block randomisation works

However, randomisation or matching doesn't mean between-subjects designs are perfect it deals with the problem of unbalanced groups. The remaining issue is that there is still a lot of variation between our groups because people are different, randomisation deals with some systematic variance but we cannot account for it all.

As you will see in chapters 11 and 12 many statistical tests are looking at variance in data accounted for by the IV compared to "noise" or error variance. Between-subjects designs have a lot of noise so to deal with this we need to recruit more participants than the alternative design – the within-subjects design.

Within-subject design (also called a repeated measures design)

In this design, our participants **experience all conditions**, so in our example, they would do the driving simulator in the alcohol and the control condition. What we are doing is looking for differences within our subjects

Within-subject design. A design where our participants experience all conditions (they are tested on the DV repeatedly).

(hence the name). The critical thing to remember in within-subjects design is that the dependent variable is measured more than once under different conditions. Students often mix within-subject designs with correlational designs (see Chapter 12) in the latter variables are measured once, and we look at associations between different variables, this is different to the within-subjects design.

In this case, we have a group of participants who undergo both the alcohol and control conditions. As you have probably already guessed, this deals with the fundamental issue that the between-subjects design has, individual differences. In within-subjects design individual differences are vastly reduced because we are comparing behaviour within the same people. This means that there are no worries about random assignment etc, as our conditions are perfectly matched on participant characteristics. This also means we have to recruit fewer participants for two reasons.

1   We don't need a different set of participants for each condition
2   These designs are more powerful because we have reduced noise (caused by individual differences that we get in between-subjects designs regardless of the clever ways that we put them in conditions).

Sound's great doesn't it? Why on earth wouldn't someone just run these designs every time? Well, the reason is they bring up a whole host of problems that have to be dealt with.

Practice effects

The more you do something, the better you become at it. This is a really big problem in within-subjects designs. If our participants did the control condition first then the alcohol condition, we might mask some of the effects of alcohol. This is because when they do the alcohol condition they will have done the simulation already, will be familiar with the task and know what is

Alcohol condition   **No alcohol condition**

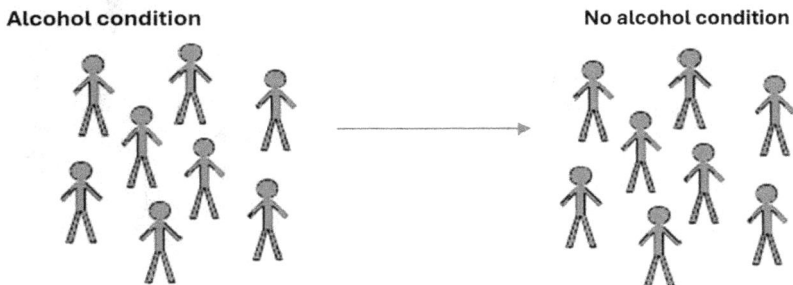

Figure 5.4 within-subjects design

expected, and they may also be less nervous as well. This is a problem in a huge range of tasks. Let's say we want to look at working memory. The first time you do the working memory task you will have to get used to task demands, rules etc. The second time you will not, so may perform better.

Fatigue/boredom effects

The other side of the coin of practice effects. If people do tasks repeatedly, they may simply become bored or tired and stop doing it to the best of their ability. This also can be exhibited in what is called response acquiesce, whereby participants just keep giving the same response; for example, you have a task where participants have to discriminate three different colours, and you end up with participants just clicking "red" throughout the entire task.

How can we fix these two problems?

We need to present things in different orders which we can do this in two ways: we can call these "complete" and "incomplete" within-subjects designs.

Complete designs: individual participants go through each of the conditions multiple times, changing the order of conditions with each administration. This should balance the practice and fatigue effects across conditions. It doesn't remove them (indeed it can increase them as they are doing the conditions multiple times) but the key thing is it makes the impact of them similar within the participants.

Incomplete designs: individual participants do the conditions in a single order, but the order is different across the participants. This is known as counterbalancing and is very common. So, in our example, some will do the alcohol and then the control condition and others will do the control and then the alcohol condition:

Alcohol condition   **No alcohol condition**

Figure 5.5 Counterbalancing

This balances out the order effects across participants. If there are more conditions then it gets more complicated. If we have three conditions e.g. alcohol, sleep deprivation, and control, then there are six possible orders (1x2x3):

1   **Alcohol** Sleep-deprived <u>Control</u>
2   **Alcohol** <u>Control</u> Sleep-deprived
3   Sleep-deprived <u>Control</u> **Alcohol**
4   Sleep-deprived **Alcohol** <u>Control</u>
5   <u>Control</u> Sleep-deprived **Alcohol**
6   <u>Control</u> **Alcohol** Sleep-deprived

So participants will complete the three conditions in one of these six orders (we can randomise them to orders).

If you have more conditions, the number of orders increases exponentially, so four conditions would mean we have 24 possible orders (1x2x3x4). You may be able to randomise people to this number of conditions but possibly not. And if you have five conditions, then you have 120 possible orders of conditions, which you are unlikely to be able to randomise everyone to. You have two options when there are a lot of possible orders. Firstly, you could randomise the orders within each participant. Secondly, you could make what is called a Latin square. In a Latin square, each condition precedes and follows each other condition once. Let's take a look at a Latin square for a four-condition experiment alcohol (ALC), sleep deprived (SD), child asking how much further repeatedly (CA), and control (CON).

1	ALC	SD	CA	CON
2	SD	ALC	CON	CA
3	CA	CON	ALC	SD
4	CON	CA	SD	ALC

ALC is preceded by nothing in row one, SD in row 2, CON in row 3 and SD in row 4. Alcohol comes before SD in row 1, before CON in row 2, before SD in row 3 and before nothing in row 4. All of the conditions follow this rule. Again, this doesn't mean that we rule out order effects like practice or fatigue within our participants, but we can say these order effects are balanced across participants.

Carry-over effects

This is when the condition "bleeds" into another condition. For example, if we gave people alcohol one day and then they completed the control condition the next day, there is a possibility that they would be hungover in the control condition. This means that the alcohol condition can affect performance in the control condition; however, the control condition is not going to cause a problem in a subsequent alcohol condition. Carry-over effects are very common with interventions that involve some sort of substance/drug, and essentially a gap between conditions is required to ensure that there can be no influence of the substance. For example, in drug trials that use repeated measures, they have what is called a "wash-out" period. However, it is not just substances that can cause carryover effects. A good example of this is when studies on responses to anxiety-inducing images use within-subjects designs. If pictures stimulate anxiety this can cause a general cognitive slowing that could slow responses to non-anxiety-inducing images so the effects are muddied (see for example Waters et al., 2005).

Participant demand

A practical issue with within-subject designs is there is a lot of demand on participants. If you have four conditions, you may be expecting your participants to turn up on four different days. That is a lot to ask and participants may drop out of the experiment leaving you with missing data.

Which do you choose then?

It depends on the IVs and DVs you intend to use. Sometimes you may measure something which you think will have little differences across participants but would show practice effects in such a case between subjects designs may be better. In another situation, you may have a variable that is likely to vary across subjects quite a lot e.g. driving ability, and you may believe that your independent variable may have very different effects depending on participant characteristics (e.g. the acute effect of alcohol), this may mean you opt for within-subjects design. Ultimately, you need to weigh up the pros and cons of the two designs when deciding on an experimental design. Also, when you read about other studies bear this in mind too, there may be ways you can critique work based on them not dealing with the problems different designs have.

Multifactorial models

We do not have to stop with just one IV in an experiment, we can have more. In this case, we have multifactorial or complex models. In these models we can look at the

Multifactorial designs. Where we have multiple factorial IVs (these can be within, between or mixture of designs).

effect of each IV in isolation and then the interaction between the two IVs. I will explain this by expanding the alcohol driving simulator example.

I think the environment in which drinks are consumed is also going to influence driving errors. I believe that if alcohol is consumed in a bar, this will increase errors compared to it being consumed in a laboratory.

I could set this up using different combinations of within and between subjects measures:

Complex between

These designs have between subject IVs only

- Alcoholic drink (two levels; alcohol, control) delivered between subjects (participants only tested under one drink condition)
- Environment (two levels; bar, laboratory) between subjects (participants only tested under one environment condition)
- DV= Errors in the driving simulator (participants contribute a single score to the data set)

Complex within

These designs have within-subject variables only:

- Alcoholic drink (two levels; alcohol, control) delivered within-subjects (participants tested under both drink conditions)
- Environment (two levels; bar, laboratory) within-subjects (participants tested under both environment conditions)
- DV= Errors in the driving simulator (with each participant contributing four scores to the data set, alcohol – bar/ alcohol-laboratory / control – bar/ control-laboratory)

Complex mixed

These designs have between-subjects and within-subject variables:

- Alcoholic drink (two levels; alcohol, control), delivered within-subjects (participants tested under both drink conditions)
- Environment (two levels; bar, laboratory) delivered between subjects (participants only tested under one environment condition)
- DV= Errors in the driving simulator (with each participant contributing two scores to the data set, once following alcohol and once following a control drink)

We can add more IVs than two, but as a rule, I do not like doing this as it makes for overly complicated hypotheses and it's really hard to estimate how many participants are needed for such studies.

When doing designs like this, it is often because we believe there will be an interaction between the independent variables that will subsequently affect the DV. In this study, the interaction will tell us whether environment and drink type work together to produce differential effects on errors in the driving simulator;

Are the effects of drink consumed on errors the same in both bar and laboratory environments OR does the effect of drink differ depending on the environment in which it was consumed?

I run this experiment on a between-subjects basis and get this pattern of results:

	Drink type			
Environment	Alcohol		Control	
Laboratory	10.20 (1.56)		3.41 (0.51)	
Bar	15.42 (4.10)		3.97 (3.55)	

Figure 5.6 Values represent errors in the driving simulator (means ±SD):

The alcohol condition has on average, more errors than the control condition. But if you look at the alcohol condition, there are substantially more errors in the bar than in the laboratory environment, and his difference is not apparent in the control condition. This suggests the IVs interact with each other to influence the DV. We will discuss interactions more in the next chapter when we move away from true experiments into quasi-experiments.

Conclusion

Experimental designs are incredibly important as they allow us to infer causality. Both between and within-subjects designs can be used in experiments, but you must choose the design that is going to test your hypothesis most accurately. Look at the advantages and disadvantages of each of the designs and think about them in the context of your variables; that way you will choose the most appropriate design. Also, when reading studies by others explore if they used the techniques for mitigating the issues with these designs, this will help with your critical appraisal. Experimental designs are an important part of quantitative research but they are not the only way we can do research. Indeed, in the next two chapters we will explore examples of non-experimental designs.

Further Reading

Gupta, U., & Verma, M. (2013). Placebo in clinical trials. *Perspectives in clinical research*, 4(1), 49–52. https://doi.org/10.4103/2229-3485.106383.

References

Christiansen, P., Jennings, E., & Rose, A. K. (2016). Anticipated effects of alcohol stimulate craving and impair inhibitory control. *Psychology of addictive behaviors: Journal of the society of psychologists in addictive behaviors*, 30(3), 383–388. http s://doi.org/10.1037/adb0000148.

Gupta, U., & Verma, M. (2013). Placebo in clinical trials. *Perspectives in clinical research*, 4(1), 49–52. https://doi.org/10.4103/2229-3485.106383.

Hearst, E. (Ed.). (2019). *The first century of experimental psychology*. Routledge.

Mutz, D. C., & Pemantle, R. (2015). Standards for experimental research: Encouraging a better understanding of experimental methods. *Journal of experimental political science*, 2(2), 192–215.

Waters, A. J., Sayette, M. A., Franken, I. H., and Schwartz, J. E. (2005). Generalizability of carry-over effects in the emotional Stroop task. *Behaviour research and therapy*, 43(6), 715–732.

Chapter 6

Quasi-experimental models

Introduction

In this chapter, we will discuss quasi-experimental designs describing why they are often necessary, as well as why we can't infer causality from such studies. First, we will focus on studies when there is an existing between-subjects factor thereby making randomisation to groups impossible. Then we will discuss time series designs where the order of manipulations cannot be counterbalanced. Finally, we will discuss what we can extrapolate from these models and contrast them with "true" experimental designs.

What is a quasi-experimental model?

Quasi means having some, but not all, the properties of something. So in the context of an experiment, **this means that we are lacking some of the properties that make something a true experiment**. This is usually:

- Where we cannot randomly assign participants to conditions
- Where we cannot counterbalance the order of our conditions

> **Quasi-experimental study.** A study where we are lacking some of the properties of a true experiment.

You will recall from the previous chapter that it is essential for a between-subjects experiment to use random assignment (or tightly matched control group), and for a within-subjects design to counterbalance the order conditions are presented. However, there are numerous situations where this cannot be done leading to the use of quasi-experiments. Let's take a look at these issues in turn.

DOI: 10.4324/9781032656564-8

Between subjects quasi-experiments: Non-equivalent groups design

Sometimes we cannot randomly allo-
cate people to between-subject conditions. It may be unethical, impossible,
or impractical to do so, this means we
have a non-equivalent group design.

> **Non-equivalent group design.** A study where we cannot randomly allocate people to between-subject conditions.

Imagine I want to conduct a study that is interested in whether chronic opiate use (e.g. heroin) is associated with cognitive deficits (e.g. memory function). I cannot randomise people into heroin users and non-users and get one group to inject heroin three times per day for a year and then have a non-using group (who would inject saline three times a day for a year – remember equivalent control groups from the last chapter!). It is completely unethical to make people heroin addicts.

In this scenario, the only thing that I could do is recruit a sample of heroin users and then a sample of non-heroin users and test their memory function. If I run this study and find that heroin users have worse memory than the controls, I cannot conclude that heroin use *causes* memory dysfunction; I can only conclude that there is an *association* between heroin use and memory dysfunction.

In Chapter 5 we looked at what we need to infer causation; how well can this study meet these criteria?

- **An association between the two variables** – I can show this!
- **Time order relationship** – I don't know that heroin use comes first and then causes memory dysfunction; maybe people with memory dysfunction are more likely to start using heroin.
- **No alternative explanation aka non-spuriousness** – There may be a huge range of factors that could account for an association other than heroin directly causing memory dysfunction. Maybe people with heroin dependence are more likely to come from severely deprived areas, have poorer access to education facilities, and therefore have poorer memory function. This is related to time order relationships as well. In this case, poorer memory functioning is likely to appear before heroin use. Another alternative explanation is that perhaps heroin users are polydrug users and exposure to other drugs is what is causing memory dysfunction.

Sometimes a between-subjects variable may be just impractical to deliver in a randomised manner. For example, let's say I develop a new method for teaching four-year-olds to read in a school, I'll call it "Superphonics". I went to my local primary school, and they agreed to let me test my new reading intervention. My hypothesis is:

"Superphonics will improve children's reading compared to standard phonics lessons".

I want to randomise students into two groups "Superphonics" vs. control (normal phonics classes). It is unlikely that the headteacher will let me do that because of the disruption it would cause. Instead, I have to randomise one class to "Superphonics" and another to the control condition. How does this influence my ability to infer causation?

- **An association between the two variables** – I can show this!
- **Time order relationship** – I don't know if my intervention improved reading; maybe the one class was better at reading than the other class before my intervention.
- **No alternative explanation aka non-spuriousness** – There may be a range of differences between the children in the two classes that could account for any difference in post-intervention reading ability. Maybe one of the classes has three particularly disruptive children in it, this could lead to poorer performance on the dependent variable (post-intervention reading ability) and/or may interfere with the intervention itself (e.g. it getting interrupted repeatedly). Maybe one class all did PE before the intervention and are more tired; again this may influence the impact of the IV and the DV.

Solutions to this problem

There is no perfect solution to these issues, particularly ruling out other possible explanations for the difference, but we can try and control for some of these possible explanations. For example, attempt to match the groups on as many factors as possible.

In our example with people with heroin dependence, we could try to match them on things that we think could systematically differ between groups. We could try and match our participants on socio-economic status; we could recruit people with heroin dependence first and then try and recruit control participants matching them as closely as possible. We could recruit heroin users who don't use other drugs (although this may be difficult as often people with heroin dependence are poly-drug users). This would enable us to say our findings are due to heroin and not other drug use.

In the Superphonics example we cannot match participants as we have been given our two groups, we could test them on characteristics we deem important and see if they are matched to understand the extent to which we can rule out other explanations. We could take this further, and add another independent variable of time (before vs. after intervention) to make a multifactorial design, this will ensure that we have a time order relationship (but does not necessarily rule out other possible causes). Before we do this, however, we will explore the within-subjects version(s) of quasi-experimental designs.

Pre-post designs (uncontrolled before-and-after studies)

This can be viewed as the within-subjects version of a quasi-experimental design. In this sort of experiment, we simply look at the DV before and after an intervention. We

> **Pre-post designs.** A study where the same variables are measured before and after an intervention or treatment (with no control group).

can use our Superphonics intervention to explore this. If I do a pre-post study, I would only have the intervention condition (i.e. there would be no control condition). I would simply look at performance change between time 1 and time 2:

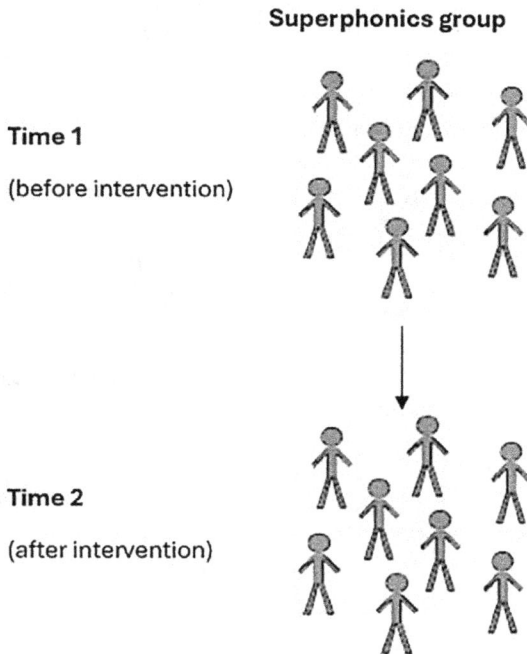

Superphonics group

Time 1

(before intervention)

Time 2

(after intervention)

Figure 6.1 Visualising pre-post designs

This sort of design does not let us infer causality as it can't meet the causal criteria of **no alternative explanation aka non-spuriousness**. This is because it lacks the control group. Any sort of reading practice may improve performance, in this design there's no way of telling if any performance improvement is due to the specific intervention. This design has a specific problem in quantitative research known as regression to the mean.

Regression to the mean

Regression to the mean occurs when one of the observations you make e.g. at time one is, for some reason, extreme (i.e. not representative of the true mean), and another observation is more representative of the true mean.

> **Regression to the mean.** When one observation is extreme (i.e. not representative) and subsequent observations are closer to the average.

For example, imagine I first tested the children on the hottest day of the year. They may be uncomfortable, irritable and distracted which would result in their reading scores at time one being very low, and not representative of their true reading ability. Then I tested them after my Superphonics intervention, and in comparison, their performance is better but this test happened to be on a standard cold UK summer day! The erroneous conclusion would be that my intervention improved performance. However, this could just be an example of regression to the mean: the intervention didn't improve anything, their performance simply went back to the mean. It looks better because our first measurement was not representative of the true mean.

In Figure 6.2 I have two measurements, 1 month before and 1 month after my Superphonics intervention (simple pre-post design). Look just how much their reading scores have gone up! I am a genius and my intervention is going to revolutionise how we teach children to read!

In Figure 6.3 I have a series of measurements both before and after my intervention (3, 2, 1 months before, and 1, 2, 3 months after). Looks like the improvement I see in Figure 6.2 is due to low scores one month before, so Superphonics did not work!

Looking at changes in within-subjects data over a long period is known as an interrupted time series design.

Interrupted time series design

This is a pretty straightforward design as it just expands upon the pre-post design. Just like in Figure 6.3 we simply expand the number of

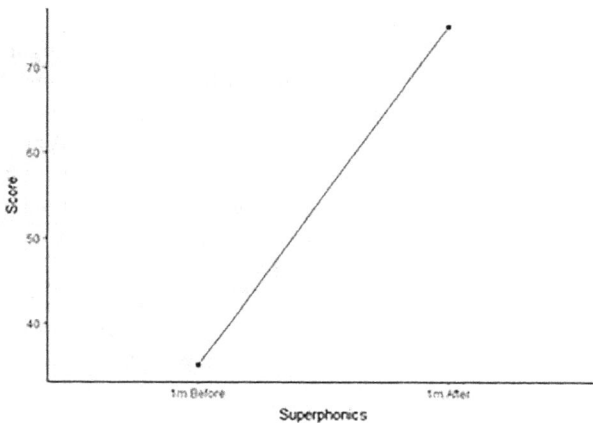

Figure 6.2 A seemingly big improvement following Superphonics!

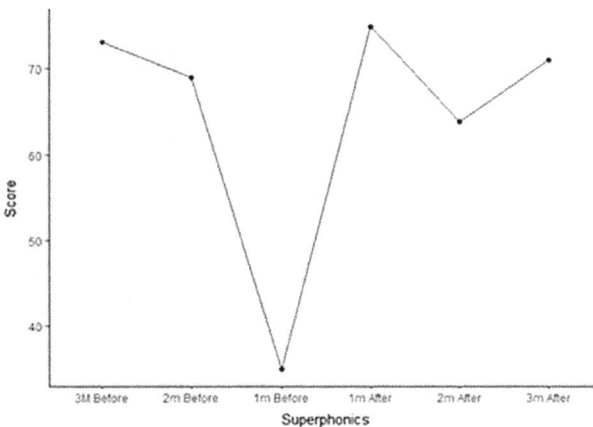

Figure 6.3 The big improvement is regression to the mean!

tests so we get a series of measures before and after the "interruption". In this case, the interruption is my Superphonics intervention.

This design is popular with nationwide interventions. For example, we may be

Interrupted time series design. A study where the same variables are measured multiple times before and after an intervention or treatment (with no control group).

interested in the effects of a sugar tax on unhealthy food consumption. We can't experiment on this as it's a new policy being introduced across the entire country so we just have to use data available to us to understand if the intervention had an impact. So we could get sales of high sugar products from supermarkets (£millions) over monthly periods as our dependent variable. Because we are aware of regression to the mean we will not just look at two time points. Instead we will look at several. Here are two figures of hypothetical data: in Figure 6.4A, the intervention appears to have had an impact, but in Figure 6.4B it has not.

Despite appearances, we cannot attribute the change seen in Figure 6.4 to the intervention. Perhaps at the same time, there was a public health campaign justifying the new legislation. This may have made people more aware of their intake and the health impacts of sugar. It could be the new tax didn't affect sales, the public health campaign did.

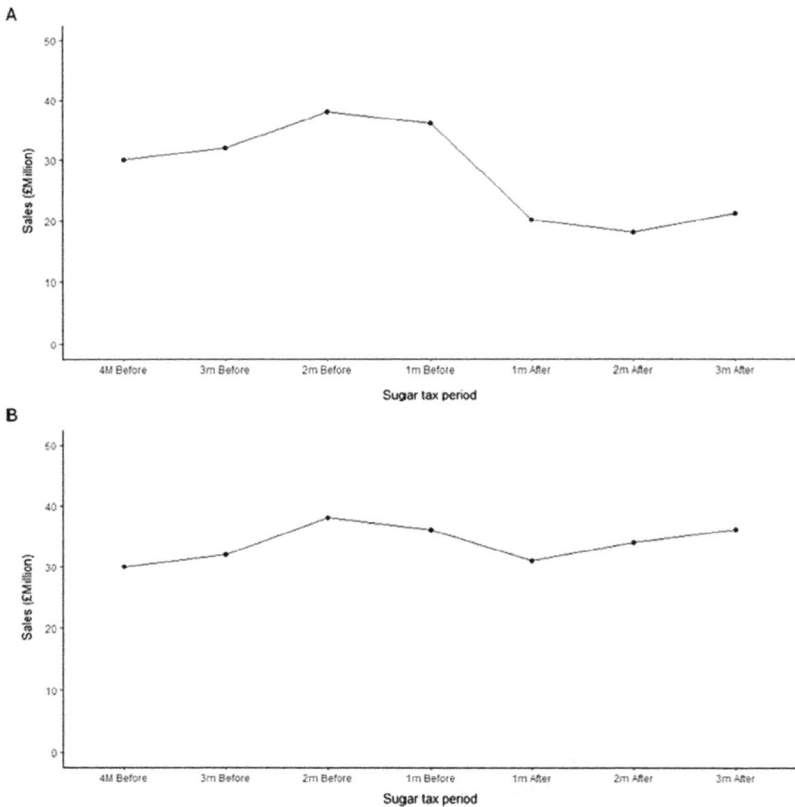

Figure 6.4 Apparent impact of legislation (A) vs. no impact (B)

Making Quasi experiments multifactorial

You will recall from the last chapter that multifactorial experiments are when we have more than one IV. We can use this method in quasi-experimental designs effectively.

Looking at the Superphonics example, we can have our intervention on a between-subjects basis (Superphonics class vs. control class) and then test the children before and after the intervention (within-subjects). This will let us know if our Superphonics intervention is improving reading and means we would be less concerned about pre-existing differences in class ability. The new independent variable would simply be "Time" (before intervention vs. after intervention). This means that we have a mixed design:

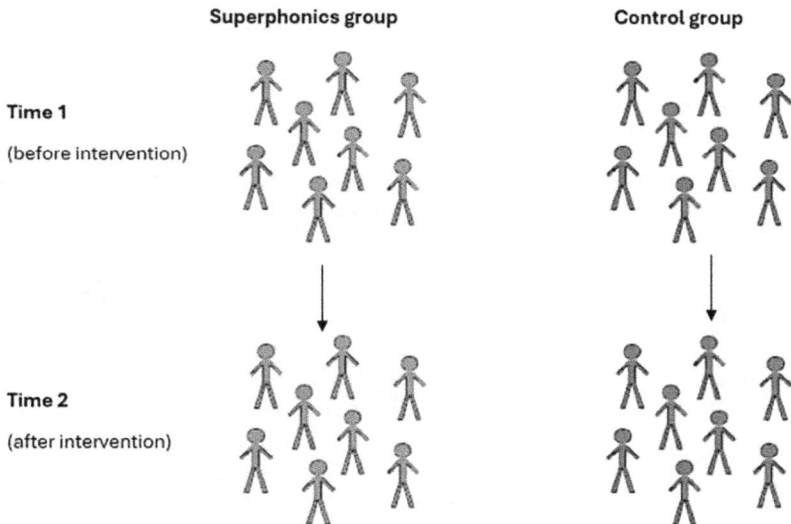

Figure 6.5 Quasi-experimental design with added repeated measures

The critical thing we would look for in this quasi-experiment is an *interaction* between time and reading conditions. We would hypothesise that the improvement in performance over time (between time one and time two) would be greater in the Superphonics class compared to the control class.

Let's look at a simple graph of the results to see what this would look like (Figure 6.6.A). As you can see, both groups are evenly matched on their reading score at 1 month before the intervention, but 1 month after the Superphonics class is better than the control class. This

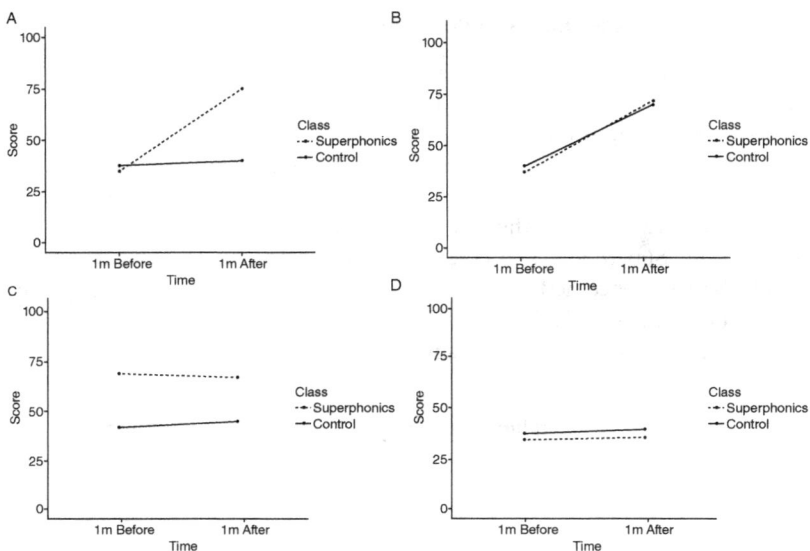

Figure 6.6 Graph showing a positive effect of super phonics (A), No effect of the intervention, but an effect of time (B), An effect of the intervention, but not across time (C) and No effects at all (D)

suggests that the intervention improved reading. However, remember this is a quasi-experiment because our participants were not randomly assigned. There could be other things that can account for the class effect. Maybe the control class got a new teacher and several of the children decided they didn't like them so stopped trying, or the children in the Superphonics class were keen and would have improved more rapidly anyway. Indeed, it is also possible that the Superphonics class are showing regression to the mean, on the day we originally tested them it may have been really hot so they were distracted, whereas the control class were tested on a cooler day.

If my intervention was no better than the usual classes the graph would look something like Figure 6.6.B. Note that the lines are parallel, suggesting the class (Superphonics vs. control) isn't having a different effect over time. Indeed, if the class type were to have an effect over time, the lines would diverge like they do in Figure 6.6.A. A differential effect of one IV depending on the levels of another IV would be evidenced by the lines diverging, converging or crossing. You will note in Figure 6.6.B that there is an effect of time, and performance increases in both groups, my Superphonics intervention does not amplify this increase as I predicted.

In Figure 6.6.C, there is an effect of class, but this class effect is not different across time. Again the lines are parallel, showing the effect of class type is not different across time. What we see here is our Superphonics class is better both before and after the Superphonics intervention than the control class. This shows why looking at the effect of an intervention over time is so important. If I had only compared the two classes after the intervention then I may have concluded that Superphonics improved outcomes, but actually, that class was better anyway, which is a fundamental problem with non-random allocation in a quasi-experimental design!

For completeness, the final graph (Figure 6.6.D) shows no effect of class or time, two flat lines almost on top of each other, reflecting no change in scores across the two conditions.

Conclusion

When conducting research, we often find ourselves in a situation where we are unable to run a true experiment i.e., we cannot randomise groups on a between-subjects basis or, in within-subjects designs, we cannot effectively counterbalance conditions. This can be for ethical reasons (we cannot randomise a group of people to have suffered childhood trauma, be dependent on drugs, or have a neurological disorder) or it can be for more practical reasons (we have only been given access to specific groups, an intervention is occurring in real life and not part of a formal experiment). This is where we use quasi-experimental designs. We need to be careful about inferring causality from such designs as we cannot know if effects are the result of preexisting differences in groups, or regression to the mean. However, if we are aware of these limitations we can try and combat them to some extent. While we cannot be certain of causal relationships we can rule out some likely alternative explanations and/ or ensure effects are not the product of things like regression to the mean.

Further Reading

Reichardt, C. S. (2009). Quasi-experimental design. *The SAGE handbook of quantitative methods in psychology*, 46–71.

West, S. G., Biesanz, J. C., & Pitts, S. C. (2000). *Causal inference and generalization in field settings: Experimental and quasi-experimental designs.*

Marsden, E., & Torgerson, C. J. (2012). Single group, pre-and post-test research designs: Some methodological concerns. *Oxford review of education*, 38(5), 583–616.

Lopez Bernal, J., Cummins, S., & Gasparrini, A. (2018). The use of controls in interrupted time series studies of public health interventions. *International journal of epidemiology*, 47(6), 2082–2093.

Chapter 7

Correlational models

Introduction

In this chapter, we will be discussing correlational designs. After reading the previous two chapters it is easy to think that we shouldn't be using designs that cannot show causality. However, this is not the case, I will discuss the role of correlational designs when an experiment is impossible or impractical (drawing parallels with quasi-experiments). The chapter will go on to discuss the role of correlational designs with big data, and how they are useful to study small, population level effects that might not be visible in an experimental design but may have an impact on society as a whole. We will then briefly discuss how we can control for variables that may confound effects.

What is correlational research?

A correlational research design is where researchers want to examine the association between two or more variables. The association being studied could be:

> **Correlational research**. Where we look for an association between two or more variables and there are no experimental manipulations.

- Cross-sectional – where variables are measured at the same time as each other.
- Longitudinal – where the variables are measured over time.

What a correlational design enables us to do is understand the direction of the relationships between variables (e.g. as one variable increases so does the other one) and the strength of the relationship between variables.

Unlike experimental research there is no manipulation of variables at all we simply collect data and then test for an association. Of course, this has

DOI: 10.4324/9781032656564-9

some crossover with quasi-experimental designs (e.g. if we compared people with a neurological disorder to those without on working memory). Indeed, it could be argued that a quasi-experimental design like that is correlational research too.

In correlational research, we cannot show causality. Let's refresh ourselves with what we need to show causality. To do this let's look through the lens of two examples:

1   *Ice cream sales cause shark attacks:* To do this I get data from ice cream sellers on beaches in Australia and the shark attack statistics for these beaches (cross-sectional).
2   *Fear of childbirth is going to be associated with postpartum anxiety:* To look at this I will measure fear of childbirth in pregnant people and then measure postpartum anxiety three months after they give birth (longitudinal).

- **An association between the two variables** – We can do this; I merely have to show there is an association between the two variables!
- **Time order relationship** – this is a fancy way of saying that variation in one of the variables must come before variation in the other. For example 1, I cannot do this, I simply have data on ice cream sales over a given period and shark attacks over the same period. There is no way I can say that people eat ice cream and then sharks attack them. For example 2, I can infer a time order relationship as they have not had a child when I measured fear of childbirth (so could not have postpartum anxiety) so I can order these variables.
- **No alternative explanation aka non-spuriousness** – I'm stuck here for both the examples. For example 1 the alternative explanation is hot weather, when it's hot people swim in the sea and buy ice creams (this is a better explanation than sharks finding humans filled with ice cream especially delicious). For example 2 there are many other explanations such as overall anxiety susceptibility causing fear of childbirth and postpartum anxiety.

So correlational research cannot show causal effects, so it's rubbish and we shouldn't do it, right? Wrong!

Why do we need correlational research?

Like in quasi-experimental designs, there is often no way that we can set up an experiment, be it due to ethical or practical reasons, this leaves us with no choice but to do correlational research. If we try to set up experiments with our previous examples we end up with massive ethical problems.

1   Ice cream sales cause shark attacks: IV- people eat three ice creams or eat three doughnuts (control condition), we then throw them in a pool containing a hungry shark and time how long it takes them to be attacked (DV). Although the first part (eating food) is pleasant enough, the next part is somewhat unethical! We certainly would need to do a between-subjects design too (I imagine we would lose a few participants the first time around).

2   Fear of childbirth is going to be associated with postpartum anxiety: IV- cause fear of childbirth in one set of expectant mothers' by telling them how awful it is vs. a standard care group, then see which group has greater postpartum anxiety.

However, sometimes we could argue that correlational research could, in some ways, be better than the experimental alternative. We will use a final example here in which I hypothesise that *gambling makes people more impulsive*. An experimental design to test this could be:

• IV – people come into the laboratory and place a series of hypothetical bets in a gambling task (I record ten horse races and make people gamble on them with pretend money) and then in another session they just watch ten horse races (within-subjects design). I measure their impulsivity computerised measure called the Stop-Signal task.

Using this I could explore causal associations but how realistic is it? Does gambling with pretend money give a true gambling experience? Perhaps impulsivity is only increased after many years of gambling, and so on. This experimental study may not be realistic enough, which means it is lacking in what we call ecological validity (which I have dedicated Chapter 13 to). So this example leaves us in a bit of a bind. Our experimental study is not realistic, but a correlational study in which I correlate how often people gamble with their performance on the Stop signal task cannot show causality. What can I do to resolve this?

Do both! Correlational research can often give us some ideas as to what we should be exploring experimentally. The two methods may end up complementing each other to give us a really firm evidence base. So, I could conduct correlational research in which I recruit gamblers, assess the length of time they have spent gambling (or indeed several indices of gambling – how much they bet per week, most they have lost, take a measure of problem gambling behaviour), and see if this correlates with performance on the Stop-Signal task. If I do find an association (step one in the stages of causality) I can then see if there is a causal relationship and set up an experiment in which I manipulate gambling (like in the example given earlier). Using these methods will enable us to converge on an answer to the research question using two different methods that have their advantages and disadvantages.

More data more (less?) problems

We live in an era of big data. By this, I mean that there is a huge amount of data available to quantitative researchers that has been collected for all manner of reasons. For example, you can go to the UK data service https://ukdataservice.ac.uk/ and find a huge amount of data for a range of things that might be of interest to you, in Figure 7.1 below you can see the themes that it covers.

You may access data through this, or one of many other websites, to answer a research question that you have in mind. This is great for researchers: someone else has already gone to the time, effort, and expense of collecting data so you don't have to! However, this also provides some problems. It may be the data has been collected in a sub-optimal way for your needs. For example, the data set may have the age of participants in "response bins" i.e. 18–23 years, 24–29 years, and so on, when you would prefer the actual age (I can't think of a situation where you would want response bins over actual ages – see Chapter 4). So this data comes with some limitations built into it. Likewise, it could be missing a variable you deem important (e.g. you may wish to account for socioeconomic status). When deciding on using such forms of data you need to think about whether these limitations make any analysis worthwhile.

Browse by theme

Ageing >	COVID-19 >	Crime >	Economics >
Environment and energy >	Education >	Ethnicity >	Food >
Health >	Housing >	Information and communication >	Labour >
Politics >	Poverty >		

Figure 7.1 UK data service themes

If you do deem the data worth using these data sets also have some advantages. Firstly, they are often very big! More data is often a very good thing as it gives us what is called "Statistical power" (more on this in Chapter 9). Essentially, by increasing power we are more likely to be able to see smaller, more subtle patterns in the data that would not be observable in small data sets.

Critically, these data sets often consist of correlational data, rather than experimental data. This means that any analyses that you do with such data sets will, more often than not, have the key limitations of correlational studies that we have discussed.

As discussed, a big advantage of these large-scale data sets is that they have the power to detect small associations. This can be potentially important. Although a really small association between two variables may appear to be trivial, tiny associations when applied at a population level (e.g. the whole country) may have a valuable impact. For example, we may have a large data set of 100,000 participants that explores the impact of removing branding from cigarette packages. Imagine this finds that this reduced smoking by 0.5%. Sounds like it doesn't work right? But if we crunch the numbers on this:

- There are approximately 6.4 million smokers in the UK (ONS, 2023)
- 0.5% of 6.4million = 32,000 less smokers.
- So that's a lot of people not smoking.
- Furthermore, smokers cost the NHS 2.6 billion per year, this would reduce spending by £13 million.

So, we can detect this small effect that may have a reasonable impact on a population level. However, because the effect of packaging is so small it would be difficult to detect in an experimental study (you would need a huge amount of participants), and again how realistic would such an experiment study be? However, even with a big data set, we are unlikely to know if there is a causal effect of the new boxes. The effect could be a product of a general downward trend in smoking, or other factors accounting for the decrease (e.g. increased "vaping").

Taking control

The fact that we cannot rule out other explanations in correlational research is problematic; however, there is something we can do (indeed we can do this in experimental and quasi-experimental designs too if necessary). We can use statistical techniques to control for the presence of variables that may account for the association we are seeing. I won't go into this in too much detail here (see Chapter 11 for more), but to briefly explain we can essentially account for the variability in our outcome.

If we think about our postpartum anxiety and fear of childbirth study, we can control for variables we think will influence postpartum anxiety (but we are not directly interested in) and see if the variable we are interested in (fear of childbirth) accounts for variability in postpartum anxiety after we have controlled for these other variables. To know what to control for you need to do reading on the subject:

- **Hypothesis:** *Fear of childbirth is going to be associated with postpartum anxiety*
- **What to control for:** Age, number of previous children, previous diagnosis of anxiety
- **What our results tell us now:** After controlling for age, number of previous children, and previous diagnosis of anxiety, there is/is not an association between fear of childbirth and postpartum anxiety.

Or for the other example:

- **Hypothesis:** Ice cream sales cause shark attacks
- **What to control for:** Temperature, average shark activity in the area, use of shark nets to protect swimmers
- **What our results tell us now:** After controlling for temperature, average shark activity in the area, and use of shark nets to protect swimmers, there is/is not an association between Ice cream sales and shark attacks.

The variables that we control for are sometimes referred to as confounding variables or nuisance variables.

Terms used in correlational research

IV? IV'e No idea

A final thing I want to cover is the language used for these designs, as things are sometimes phrased differently. It is important to remember that correlational research has no manipulation; this is why sometimes people do not refer to IVs and DVs in this sort of research, sometimes they call them predictors and outcomes (respectively). For example, if I hypothesised that gambling made people more impulsive, I could measure how long participants have been gambling (the predictor) and then give them an impulsivity task (e.g. the Stop-Signal task; outcome).

Independent variable = Predictor
Dependent variable = Outcome

> **Predictor variable.** Predictor variable - The variable we are using to predict change in the outcome (correlational version of the independent variable).

Often, there is no clear predictor and an outcome instead we are exploring associations in a broad way, e.g. if I hypothesise that two personality traits (extraversion and sensation seeking) are associated with each other. In this case, I would not really be able to call one a predictor and an outcome, they would both simply be called variables.

Effects and associations

Also, you must avoid using the word "effect" when writing up correlational work. Effect suggests causality; A effects B means when A changes we see a subsequent change in B. Instead in correlational research, we should talk about A being associated with B as this is a non-causal statement and does not mislead.

> **Outcome variable.** The variable we are looking for change in (correlational version of the dependent variable).

Conclusion

Correlational studies are a key part of quantitative research; personally, I spend over half my time doing correlational research. Although such studies cannot allow us to infer causality this does not mean they are not of value. They are really important when ethical or practical issues mean we cannot set up an experiment. Furthermore, you can also view them as a piece of the puzzle and use them in conjunction with experimental work to make more robust inferences. Finally, when doing correlational research make sure that you say association not effect, you will often read papers that are inferring causality and using causal language when they shouldn't!

Further Reading

Lau, F. (2017). Methods for correlational studies. In *Handbook of ehealth evaluation: An evidence-based approach* [*internet*]. University of Victoria.

Kite, M. E., & Whitley, B. E. (2018). Correlational designs. In *Principles of Research in Behavioral Science* (pp. 432–465). Routledge.

References

Gov.uk. *Research and analysis – Cost of smoking to the NHS in England: 2015* [Internet]. Public Health England. (2017) [cited 2021 Sep 30]. Available at: https://www.gov.uk/government/publications/cost-of-smoking-to-the-nhs-in-england-2015/cost-of-smoking-to-the-nhs-in-england-2015.

Office for National Statistics. *Adult smoking habits in the UK: 2022.* (2023) https://www.ons.gov.uk/peoplepopulationandcommunity/healthandsocialcare/healthandlifeexpectancies/bulletins/adultsmokinghabitsingreatbritain/2022.

Chapter 8

Sampling theory

Introduction

Following the previous three chapters on research design, we will now move on to sampling, i.e. who (or what) is going to be in a study. First, we will look at the common language of samples, clearly defining what populations, sampling frames, and samples are, and how they relate to each other. It will then describe sampling theory and how it allows us to understand who you can extrapolate findings to, and the importance of a sample that will represent the population of interest.

Sampling

You're walking around a supermarket and you see one of the store assistants on a stand with a new type of crisp. You are allowed to try one or two and from this small taster, you can decide if you want to buy them. You do this under the assumption that the sample will taste the same as the product that you will buy.

Sampling in research generally follows this logic; we take a small sample of people and use that to extrapolate to people we have not sampled. We are doing this under the assumption that the sample we take represents the population that we have sampled them from.

When sampling foods we can be pretty sure what we taste will be like what we purchase, but with sampling in quantitative research, we cannot necessarily be sure that our sample represents the population we have sampled them from. To understand sampling we need to discuss a few concepts first: population, sampling frame and the sample.

Population

The population refers to the complete group of people/animals/elements that you are interested in

Population. The complete group you are interested in studying.

DOI: 10.4324/9781032656564-10

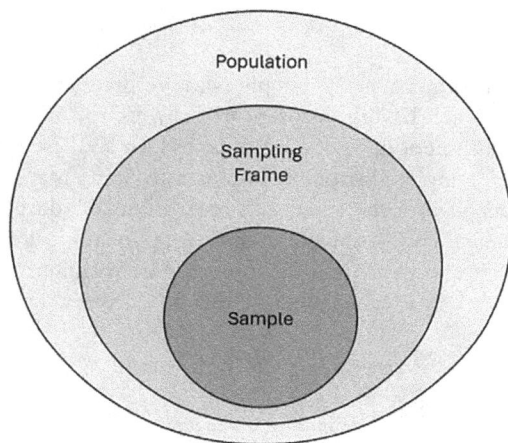

Figure 8.1 Population, sampling frame, and sample

studying. The population of interest to you will be defined by specific characteristics that will make it distinguishable from another population. This means that your population will have a defined scope, i.e. you will identify the terms of what makes up your population of interest. Populations can be diverse/heterogenous (e.g. children born in the UK since 2020) or similar/homogenous (e.g. Females under 25 who have experienced COVID-19 symptoms in the last month). A population could be humans, animals, objects or events.

It is important that you can define your population clearly as this will help with sampling. It will also allow you to make precise generalisations from your sample to the population.

Table 8.1 Examples of populations

Human Populations	Animal population	Objects	Events
All students in your university	All ex-racing greyhounds in the UK	All iPhones made in 2022	All shipping accidents in the South China Sea

Sampling frame

The sampling frame exists within the population. **It's a list that contains members of the population of interest.** This does not mean it is exactly the same as the population though. Let's go back to an example in the Chapter 7;

Sampling frame. A list that contains members of the population of interest (not necessarily all of them).

"Fear of childbirth is going to be associated with postpartum anxiety"

For this, my population may be people who are pregnant in the Liverpool City region and are having scans at the Liverpool Women's Hospital during a six-month period. I get a list of emails for all these people, but it is unlikely to be a complete list of my population. Some may not have given their contact details in, others may not have an email address. This means that my sampling frame is not my complete population, it is smaller. The sampling frame is essentially people who *could* be recruited.

Let's take a look at another example this time from Chapter 6:

"Superphonics will improve children's reading compared to standard lessons".

If you recall, this example involved me going into a school and having one class do the Superphonics intervention and another doing standard classes. In this case, my sampling frame is quite small, as it is children on the register for the classes that I am allowed to test. My sampling frame differs dramatically from my population of interest which is 4–5-year-old school children in the UK.

Sample

The sample is simply people who have been recruited for the study and is a subset of the sampling frame. There are many reasons why you would not recruit a full sampling frame. Firstly, you may deem you need a certain number of people to get the statistical power (Chapter 9) to be able to detect an effect of interest. It would often be completely impractical to recruit an entire sampling frame as well as it could run into the many thousands of possible participants. The sample not being the same as the sampling frame may be for things outside of the researcher's control e.g. people may not want to take part or there may be an error in the contact details.

Sample. The people who have been recruited for a study.

In the postpartum anxiety study the sample will differ from the sampling frame because I may not need to recruit the full sample, and some of those who I approach may not want to take part in the study. Likewise, in the Superphonics study some children may be absent, they may switch schools, or perhaps their parents don't want them to do it so don't give consent.

Let's look at the population, sampling frame and sample for the Superphonics study in a diagram:

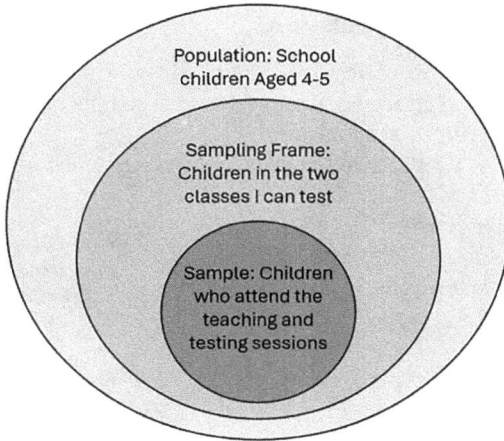

Figure 8.2 Population, sampling frame, and sample for the for the Superphonics study

Here's another example, based on that in Chapter 5 where we wanted to explore the effects of alcohol on driving performance.

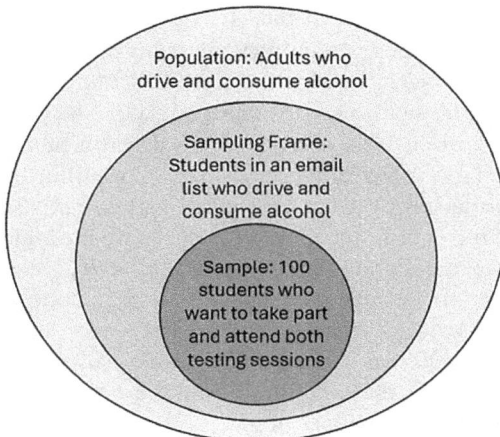

Figure 8.3 Population, sampling frame, and sample for the for the alcohol and driving study

Linking samples to populations

We want to be able to extrapolate findings from a sample to the population. When thinking about population data and sample data there are some things you will need to keep in mind.

Firstly, there is a difference between a parameter and a statistic.

- **A parameter is a number that describes a property of an entire *population***
- **A statistic is a number that describes a property of a *sample***

> **Parameter.** A number that describes a property of an entire population.

This may seem like a picky distinction, but it is important to understand. Take a simple example, age.

- If I was able to get the age of everyone in the UK I could calculate the mean age of the UK, this would be a parameter.
- If I randomly select 10,000 people in the UK and calculate their mean age, this would be a statistic.

> **Statistic.** A number that describes a property of a sample.

Usually, we deal with statistics. In the Superphonics study in Figure 8.1, the population is all children in the UK aged between 4 and 5. It's not possible to recruit all children and get the population parameter instead I have to recruit a *sample* of children from which I can get statistics.

Sometimes, it is possible to get an entire population. Maybe I am interested in the scores on a work satisfaction scale in my department, my population of interest is all staff in the University of Liverpool's Department of Psychology. In this case, it is feasible to recruit the entire population. However, usually, populations are too large to recruit all of them, so we use samples.

So, when we are conducting a study and get statistics from our sample we want to be able to make inferences about the population from them. This means that you want to ensure that your sample represents the population as much as possible, so you can extrapolate from it. This is where the sampling technique becomes important, and why I am dedicating an entire chapter to it (see Chapter 10).

For now, let's assume that you have a representative sample (i.e. it reflects your population of interest). We use inferential statistics to make educated guesses about the population. However, because our sample is not the full population we have what we call sampling error (which would be the difference between the unknown parameter and the sample statistics). The size of this error depends on your sample size and your recruitment method.

This means that when we make estimates about a population we get two types of statistics. A point estimate (i.e. the estimated parameter) e.g. "the average age of my sample is 42", and a range of values in which there is an expectation that the parameter will lie (most often a confidence interval – Chapter 9) suffice to say they take sampling error into account.

Central Limit Theorem (CLT)

CLT states that, given a sufficiently large sample, the sampling distribution of the sample mean will be approximately normally distributed, regardless of the *original distribution of the population.* A normal distribution is simply an inverted U- or bell-shaped curve like below.

> **Central Limit Theorem (CLT) & normal distribution.** The fact that the distribution of the sample mean (in a sufficiently large sample) will be normally distributed regardless of the population's original distribution, if the samples are independent and identically distributed.

This holds provided the samples are independent, meaning the selection of one sample does not influence the selection of another, and is identically distributed (each sample is drawn from the same population and follows the same probability distribution). This means that we can use statistical tests to make inferences about data.

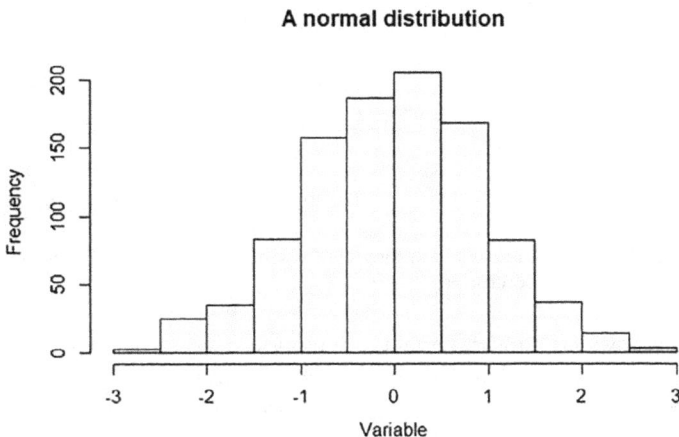

A normal distribution

Figure 8.4 A normal distribution

Imagine I am looking at postpartum anxiety in new mothers and I have a population with anxiety scores between 0 and 10 and this does not have a normal distribution. Like in the figure below:

Histogram

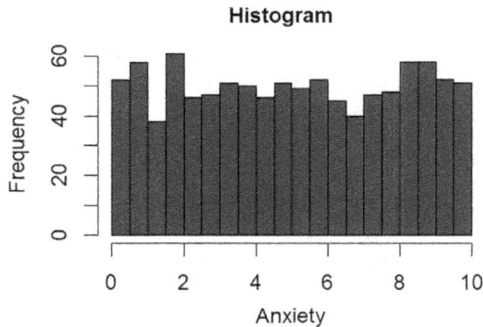

Figure 8.5 A population of a non-normally distributed population

Now if I take 500 samples of 30 participants from this population and plot the mean of these samples, I get a normal distribution:

Distribution of Sample Means

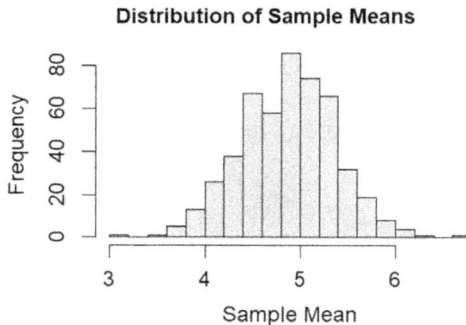

Figure 8.6 The distribution of the means of 500 samples taken from my non-normally distributed population

This allows us, under certain assumptions about the data, to make inferences about population parameters. Furthermore, this facilitates several methods of hypothesis testing using statistics.

Conclusion

Understanding the basics of sampling theory is critical to quantitative methods in psychology. The hierarchy of population to sampling frame to the sample is a good way of thinking about the data that you are going to collect. When we move on to specific methods we will have a chapter on how you best recruit a sample to ensure it represents the population (Chapter 10). Remember the aim is to apply sample statistics to populations, i.e. make our sample and findings speak to the real world.

Further Reading

Wroughton, J. R., McGowan, H. M., Weiss, L. V., & Cope, T. M. (2013). Exploring the role of context in students' understanding of sampling. *Statistics Education Research Journal*, 12(2), 32–58.

Wu, C., & Thompson, M. E. (2020). *Sampling theory and practice*. Cham: Springer International Publishing.

Chapter 9

Null Hypothesis Significance Testing (NHST)

Introduction

We are now going to look at key statistical concepts in quantitative research. Firstly, it will discuss the concept of NHST and the role of p values in testing hypotheses, drawing upon the examples used in previous chapters. The role of power (sample size) in NHST will be described in terms of its influence on p values. In describing the dangers with NHST there, we will discuss over interpretation of what p values mean and logical fallacies. Next, the concept of effect size will be described before a discussion about confidence intervals and their interpretation, linking them to NHST.

Testing hypotheses with statistics

We have talked a lot about hypotheses in previous chapters, however, we have not discussed how we use quantitative methods to test them. Strap yourselves in, get a tea or coffee, and let's get stuck into something that is often misunderstood!

More often than not when we test hypotheses we do it through the Null Hypothesis Significance Testing (NHST) framework. We know what hypotheses are, they are things that sound like this:

> *"Consuming alcohol will increase the number of errors in a driving simulator compared to a placebo alcohol condition"*

A null hypothesis sounds like this:

> *"There will be no difference in errors between the alcohol and placebo conditions"*

DOI: 10.4324/9781032656564-11

Which we can distil down to:

"The means of the groups will not be different"

Null hypotheses are simple since they say groups won't be different or there will not be an association between variables (in the case of correlational research). A key point that we need to remember is that when we do NHST, it is done from the perspective of the *null hypothesis being true.*

Probability

In NHST we produce a probability value referred to as a p-value for our hypothesis test. The p-value is a value that ranges from 0 (no chance of this happening) to 1 (this is certainly happening), as such it can also be thought about as a % (e.g. p =1 is 100%, p=0 is 0%, p =.05 is 5%, p =.001 is .01% and so on).

Now, when we test our hypothesis we are looking at probability in terms of our collected data and the null hypothesis. The null hypothesis in our example is, *"Means of the groups will not be different"*. We look at the collected data from our experiment in which one group of people were given alcohol and another a placebo drink, and we then recorded errors during a driving simulation. Here's the data we collected:

Table 9.1 Driving simulation data, values are the number of errors

Alcohol	Placebo
10	6
8	5
12	5
4	8
8	5
9	8
12	10
14	11
15	8
16	8
17	7
10	7
5	9
4	8
6	6

To test the hypothesis, we are asking, "*How likely is it that I would find data like this if the null hypothesis is true*".

The probability we produce from our statistical analysis is a *conditional probability* – the condition being that the null hypothesis is true! If we hope to find a difference then we want the p-value to be small, which means the probability of getting data like this, if no difference exists, is small (unlikely).

So if I run a t-test (more on this in Chapter 12) to compare the two groups in Table 9.1 I get a p-value of.043 (p=.043), this means that if there is no difference between groups (alcohol does not have an effect of driving errors – my null hypothesis), then the likelihood of me getting this p-value is 4.3% (or 4.3/100) so not particularly likely at all; but is this small probability enough to say that we have supported the hypothesis?

Cutt-offs (not the trousers)

Generally, the cut-off for saying a result is "statistically significant" (i.e. there is a statistically significant difference between the alcohol and placebo conditions in the number of driving errors) is a p-value of less than .05 (written as p<.05). This as a percentage is 5%, or as a fraction it is 1 in 20. So to show suport for our hypothesis we need a p-value less than .05 (p<.05).

Why do we use this value? For no good reason! It comes down to a throwaway comment by Fisher (1926) when discussing probability. Notably, he followed it up with "If one in twenty does not seem high enough odds, we may, if we prefer it, draw the line at one in fifty or one in a hundred."

So you will read a lot about p<.05 being the cut-off for statistical significance but please bear in mind that this cut-off is not the be-all and end-all! In fact, it's somewhat weak evidence! Later on in this chapter, we will discuss some issues with p values and other ways we can look at quantitative data to give us a better understanding of it.

Probability distribution: A fun(fair) example

Imagine you go to a funfair and there are all sorts of wonderful prizes like gigantic teddy bears. The games at the funfair all say that there's a 50% chance of winning, we can test if this claim is true using probability.

To do this I played ten games and I won one game. If the games truly are 50/50 the probability of this happening is **.0098** and I would sit in the bar that is second from the left in Figure 9.1. If I won five then I would be in the middle, tallest bar of Figure 9.1 (probability of **0.246**), this is what we would predict if there being a 50% chance of winning were true. Generally, we would be prepared to believe games are *not* rigged (actually 50% chance of winning) if the p-value is greater than .05.

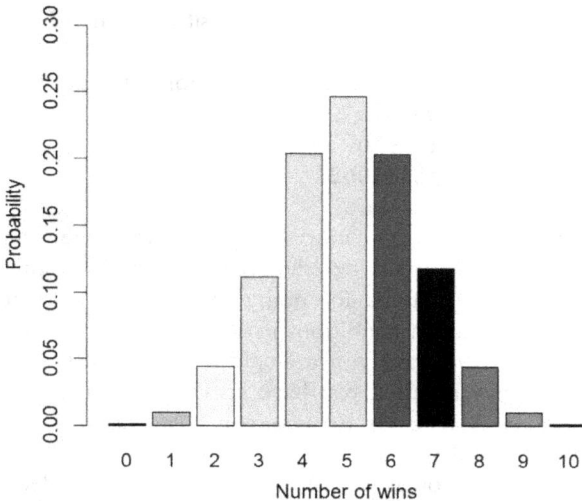

Figure 9.1 Probability distribution for playing 10 games with a 50% chance of winning

I've probably made a mistake

P values should come with some warnings! It is very easy to make mistakes with them; let's consider some:

More testing, more problems

The more testing that you do the more likely to find a significant p-value!

If you roll a fair dice you have a 1/6 chance of rolling a 6. Imagine someone says to you if you roll the dice once and get 6 you get £100. You roll the dice, and get a six! You have won, you had that 1/6 chance. Now imagine you fail to get that 6, but you keep on rolling the dice (if you keep rolling the dice you will get a 6 eventually, although *technically* this is not guaranteed!). So, after 15 rolls you finally get a six! The person who promised the money is probably going to refuse to give you the money, your six after 15 rolls is not the same as a six after one roll; the rules state you roll the dice once!

We can think about our p values a bit like this. If we do keep producing p values then we are more likely to find a statistically significant (p<.05) result by chance. This is called a false positive or a type 1 error, and this is where we incorrectly reject the null hypothesis when it is true (false positive).

We can work out the likelihood of false positives with a simple formula:

1 test: 1-.95 =.05 (i.e. our critical p-value for statistical significance)
2 tests: $1-(.95)^2 = .0975$
3 tests: $1-(.95)^3 = .142926$
4 tests: $1-(.95)^4 = .181450625$

The more times you test, the more likely you are to find a statistically significant p-value. This must be effectively dealt with. Solutions to this issue depend on the reasons for doing multiple tests. Sometimes it's because you have loads of conditions to compare, if that's the case there are statistical tests that give you a single p-value across all conditions; and if that is significant then you have justification for comparing individual conditions. Maybe it's because you have loads of variables and you correlate them all with each other. In this case, you have a big risk of false positives and you may wish to change what you deem as being statically significant, perhaps p<.01 or p<.001. Another method is called a Bonferroni correction where your cut-off for statistical significance is p .05 divided by the number of comparisons made, e.g. if you do five comparisons you would only say you have found a statistically significant result if your p-value is below .01 (.05/5).

More participants: more or less problems?

P values are essentially the product of two things, the size of an effect, (e.g. how different our groups are, or in correlational studies the strength of the association between variables) and *the size of the sample.* As your sample size increases, the influence of random error (i.e. people just being a bit different) is lessened. With bigger samples, the variance in the sample is also decreased; remember the variance formula from Chapter 4?

$$\sigma^2 = \frac{\Sigma(X - \bar{X})^2}{n - 1}$$

The n-1 bit below means "divided by the sample size -1". This means that bigger samples have less variance than small samples and the statistics from them are a more precise representation of the population. This means that with bigger samples you are more likely to find a statistically significant effect.

So if we did our drinking and driving errors study twice, once with 15 participants in each condition and another time with five in each condition as per Table 9.2.

Both groups have the same mean difference, we can see more errors (2.6 more on average in both experiments) after alcohol. However, my small sample with big variances finds this difference is not significant, whereas it is when my sample is bigger. So, small samples are less likely to find statistically significant differences. This is referred to as a lack of power. Power refers to the ability to detect a predetermined effect. If a study is underpowered, it is unlikely to find an effect. Before doing studies, people often (and should!) do an *a priori* power calculation, which identifies how big their sample will need to be based on (1) the study design, (2) the magnitude of the effect they expect to see, (3) the level of statistical significance (usually .05).

Table 9.2 15 participants vs 5 participants

Alcohol	Placebo
10	4
8	3
12	5
4	4
8	4
9	8
12	10
14	11
15	6
16	8
17	0
10	5
5	10
4	4
6	2

Alcohol	Placebo
10	2
5	6
9	7
15	8
11	14

Alcohol condition:
Mean=10, variance=13

Placebo condition:
Mean=7.4, variance=18.8

p-value for the difference:
p=.337

Alcohol condition:
Mean=10, variance=18.29

Placebo condition:
Mean=7.4, variance=3.26

p-value for the difference:
p=.043

It's significant! So what?

The word "significant" is problematic, in my opinion as it leaves the naïve reader to believe that it means results are important (when I say naïve readers I include some quite experienced researchers I have worked with). But significant results aren't necessarily meaningful. As stated above, when you have massive samples lots of things are going to have significant associations/ differences as p values are dependent on sample size (bigger samples = smaller p). Therefore, you cannot say if something is statistically significant it *matters*. For example, there is a big difference between *clinical* significance and *statistical* significance.

Imagine I developed a new form of treatment for depression and tested it on 20 patients. I measured their depression using the Beck Depression Inventory (Beck et al., 1996), and compared this to their Beck Depression Inventory scores after two weeks of my treatment. Here are the results:

Table 9.3 Beck depression inventory scores before and after treatment

Before	After
35	34
32	31
42	40
35	32
43	37
40	42
35	32
34	33
37	33
45	41
40	38
39	40
40	39
45	42
40	41

I analysed the difference between the two conditions, and found there's a highly significant difference between the two conditions (p=.006). So, my treatment is effective! Well, there is an issue with this, although scores generally go down in the participants. The cut-off for severe depressive symptoms in the Beck depression inventory is 30, so all my participants still have severe depressive symptoms after my treatment. So, can I say I produced a clinically significant improvement? No! Whether a statistically significant difference "matters" is hard to pin down, and will depend on the subject knowledge of the thing being studied.

The difference between significant and non-significant is not necessarily significant!

This may sound confusing but it is a simple concept. Let's go back to the Superphonics example. Imagine I don't know what I am doing and look at the change in reading scores in my Superphonics condition from baseline to post-intervention, and find a statistically significant improvement in their reading p=.044. Then in the control group, I looked at their reading ability over the same period (baseline to post-intervention), and this group did not show a significant improvement in their reading p=.058. I may be tempted to say Superphonics is significantly better than normal teaching as it produced a significant improvement. However, I cannot say this!

As you can see in Table 9.4 the Superphonics groups' p-value is just below the threshold for statical significance (i.e. it is just less than .05), whereas the control group is just above the threshold (i.e. it is just above .05; see Table 9.5). If I were to calculate a change score in each of the conditions, i.e. Post-intervention minus baseline scores, then compare these scores across conditions these change scores are not significantly different (Table 9.6).

Table 9.4 Change over time in the Superphonics group

Superphonics Baseline	Superphonics after intervention	Difference (Superphonics)
10	12	2
11	16	5
13	14	1
12	15	3
14	17	3
14	18	4
15	18	3
16	20	4
16	17	1
20	23	3

Difference between baseline and after intervention is significant!

p=.044

Table 9.5 Change over time in the control group

Control Baseline	Control after intervention	Difference (Control)
16	18	2
16	20	4
10	14	4
11	11	0
13	15	2
12	15	3
14	16	2
17	18	1
13	15	2
12	14	2

Difference between baseline and after intervention is significant!

p=.059

Table 9.6 Change scores compared between the two conditions

Difference (Superphonics)	Difference (Control)
2	2
5	4
1	4
3	0
3	2
4	3
3	2
4	1
1	2
3	2

Difference between the difference scores is not significant!

p=0.230

Taken together this shows me that although there is a significant improvement in the Superphonics group and not in the control group. The change in reading ability is not significantly different across groups.

(Effect) Size matters

We shouldn't only think about p values when assessing our results. Remember big samples are more likely to find significant effects, not

Effect sizes. A standardised measure of the magnitude of a given effect.

because they find larger differences or associations between variables, but because p values get smaller when sample size increases. For example, let's think about our driving simulator experiment. Two separate researchers ran experiments to find out if alcohol compared to placebo resulted in more driving errors we can use the example from earlier in this chapter (data shown again in Table 9.7).

- Experiment 1: a significant effect of alcohol on errors, p=.043.
- Experiment 2: no significant effect of alcohol on errors, p=.337.

One result is significant, the other is non-significant. However, the difference between the means of the conditions in the two experiments is the same. Essentially, no significant difference is detectable in 5 participants, but it is in 15.

One thing we can do is give effect sizes along with p values. **Effect sizes are a standardised measure of the magnitude of a given effect.** Effect size is now necessary in statistics reporting.

The American Psychological Association (APA) Task Force on Statistical Inference (Wilkinson & the APA Task Force on Statistical Inference, 1999) argued that you should:

"Always provide some effect size estimate when reporting a p-value" (p. 399).

Let's go back to the driving example and the data we looked at before: this time I am going to discuss the effect size for the two data sets (in this case it's using a statistic called Cohen's *d*)

The effect size (in this case Cohen's *d*) is similar across the groups as the means in each of the conditions of the two samples are the same, and the

Table 9.7 15 participants vs 5 participants

Alcohol	Placebo
10	4
8	3
12	15
4	4
8	4
9	8
12	10
14	11
15	6
16	8
17	0
10	5
5	10
4	4
6	2

Alcohol	Placebo
10	2
5	6
9	7
15	8
11	14

Alcohol condition:
Mean=10, variance =13

Placebo condition:
Mean=7.4, variance =18.8

P value for the difference:
p=.337

Cohens *d* =.65

Alcohol condition:
Mean=10, variance=18.29

Placebo condition:
Mean=7.4, variance=3.26

P value for the difference:
p=.043

Cohens *d* =.79

slightly different variances produce the difference in the d statistic. As effect sizes are standardised this means we can make cross-study comparisons. It's harder to do this with p-values: if one study found a significant result and another one did not, this could simply be due to sample size.

We should be in the habit of reporting p-values and effect sizes. It is important to note that there are lots of different effect sizes for different designs and data types, so the effect size that is reported depends on your specific study. Furthermore, often when people talk about effect sizes they use the terms small, medium, and large, there is some debate about these cut-offs, and the validity of having strict cutpoints (a big effect in one area of psychology may be a small effect in another area!).

We need confidence (intervals)

One final thing in our quantitative toolkit that we need to discuss is confidence intervals. P-values and effect sizes are a single estimate of the probability or size of an effect respectively. However, we can also think about how confident we are in an effect (or a given value). **This is what confidence intervals do, they give you a range of values: an upper confidence interval and a lower confidence interval (derived from your data) between which the population parameter being estimated should fall.** It is a measure of precision, the narrower the confidence intervals the more precise the estimate is. Notably, confidence intervals narrow as the sample size increases.

Confidence intervals. A range of values, an upper and a lower confidence interval (derived from your data) expressing the uncertainty around the population parameter being estimated with a specified level of confidence, usually 95%.

We choose the width of confidence intervals ourselves, and they are usually set to 95% (less commonly 99% and 90%), and are reported as "95%CI". The reason they are set to 95% is that this gives a 5% error rate (i.e. accept a 5% chance that the intervals given do not contain the true parameter). Remember the 5% error rate? That's what we used for "statistical significance" when assessing p values.

Let's imagine I am measuring postpartum anxiety. I assess participants with the postpartum specific anxiety scale (PSAS; Fallon et al 2016), and the average score is 18 with confidence intervals between 15 and 21. This would mean that I am 95% confident that the true PSAS score of the population is between 15 and 21. This example is for confidence intervals for the mean. However, confidence intervals can be done for all manner of inferential statistics. Let's take a look at my Superphonics example from before when I looked at the test scores before and after intervention for my Superphonics and control conditions separately.

Table 9.8 Change over time in the Superphonics group

Superphonics Baseline	Superphonics after intervention	Difference (Superphonics)
10	12	2
11	16	5
13	14	1
12	15	3
14	17	3
14	18	4
15	18	3
16	20	4
16	17	1
20	23	3
Mean of the difference column		2.9

Difference between baseline and after intervention is significant!

p=.044

The mean difference is 2.9

The 95% confidence intervals for the mean difference are 0.09 to 5.71

Table 9.9 Change over time in the control group

Control Baseline	Control after intervention	Difference (Control)
16	18	2
16	20	4
10	14	4
11	11	0
13	15	2
12	15	3
14	16	2
17	18	1
13	15	2
12	14	2
Mean of the difference column		2.2

Difference between baseline and after intervention is not significant!

p=0.059

The mean difference is 2.2

The 95% confidence intervals for the mean difference are -0.09 to 4.49

As we know, the interval provides a range of values within which we expect the true parameter to lie with 95% confidence. Whether or not this interval contains zero has specific implications in hypothesis testing, particularly regarding the null hypothesis (although for some situations e.g. when predicting the likelihood of being in one of two groups this specific rule doesn't apply).

If our null hypothesis that there is no difference between groups i.e. the difference between before and after scores is 0, and we get confidence intervals that do not contain 0 like for the Superphonics group where our 95% CI are 0.09 to 5.71, then the p-value is also going to be statistically significant. This is because within 95% of potential values the true parameter is not 0 (i.e. what the null hypothesis is). We know that our differences will be significant at the 0.05 level (100%-95%=5%; which as a probability is .05). If we look at the control condition then 95% CIs are -0.09 to 4.49 which contain 0 so within our potential values there is no difference (what the null is).

This means that as well as being useful to give an estimation of the range of values in which the population parameter lies, it is also linked with p values (and the concept of statistical significance).

Conclusion

This chapter is a lot to take in, and if you feel overwhelmed, don't worry about it! Loads of people struggle with NHST. Indeed, if I walk out of my office now and ask the next lecturer I see to explain NHST I reckon there's a decent chance they won't be explaining it correctly and possibly even catastrophically misinterpret it! The same also goes for confidence intervals! Effect size is a much easier thing to understand though, indeed people often, and erroneously, think about p values in terms of effect size (i.e. seeing a small p-value and thinking this means there's a big difference between groups – only effect size tells you this). All of these things are part of the quantitative researcher's toolkit and should be used to understand quantitative data.

Further Reading

Karpe, K. (2017). In chase of statistically significant result. Consequences of widespread use of NHST (null hypothesis significance testing) in psychology. In *Nauka*, 143–156.

Valentine, J. C., Aloe, A. M., & Lau, T. S. (2015). Life after NHST: How to describe your data without "p-ing" everywhere. *Basic and applied social psychology*, 37(5), 260–273.

Nickerson, R. S. (2000). Null hypothesis significance testing: A review of an old and continuing controversy. *Psychological methods*, 5(2), 241.

References

Beck, A. T., Steer, R. A., & Brown, G. (1996). Beck depression inventory–II. *Psychological assessment*.

Fallon, V., Halford, J. C. G., Bennett, K. M., & Harrold, J. A. (2016). The postpartum specific anxiety scale: development and preliminary validation. *Archives of women's mental health*, 19, 1079–1090.

Fisher, R. A.The arrangement of field experiments. *Journal of the Ministry of Agriculture of Great Britain*1926; 33:503–513.

Section 3

Key Methodologies: Which research techniques are typically used for research on this topic

Section 3 moves on to some practicalities of quantitative methods, looking at sampling methods before moving on to giving an overview of statistical tests

At the end of Section 3, you will:

3.1 Understand the different sampling methods that can be used and their advantages and disadvantages.

3.2 Become familiar with different methods of testing for associations between variables and how to interpret findings.

3.3 Become familiar with different methods of testing for differences between groups and how to interpret findings.

DOI: 10.4324/9781032656564-12

Chapter 10

Sampling methods

Introduction

This chapter will focus on sampling. Firstly, we will discuss probabilistic sampling methods and the advantages and disadvantages of these strategies linking them back to the extent to which they allow us to make inferences about effects in a population. Next, we will discuss non-probabilistic sampling and its substantial limitations (as well as strategies to counter these limitations) which, again, will be linked back to making inferences about effects in a population. Finally, I will link this to the concept of statistical power and how it influences our ability to see effects in a study, using examples from previous chapters.

Getting your sample

Back in Chapter 8, we looked at sampling theory and dealt with the concepts of a population, sampling frame and a sample. See Figure 10.1

We get our sample from our population, and the most important thing is that we get a sample that is *representative* of our population. We want the sample to be a little version of the population. For example, we would not want our sample to be much younger than the population of interest, or missing a sizeable ethnic group in the population. Therefore we need to use sampling techniques that ensure representation. A representative sample is critical if we want to get generalizable, and unbiased, results. To achieve this, we need to use probability sampling.

Probability sampling

Probability sampling is a method of selecting a sample from a population so that everyone in the population has a non-zero chance of being included in

Probability sampling. a method of selecting a sample so that everyone in the population has a non-zero chance of being included in the sample.

DOI: 10.4324/9781032656564-13

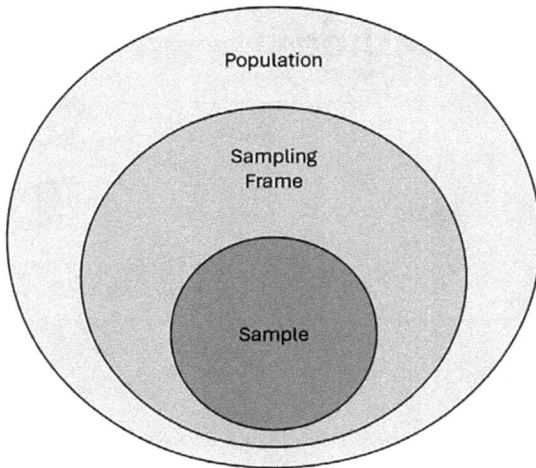

Figure 10.1 Population, sampling frame, and sample

the sample. Indeed, we should be able to work out the probability of a given person being sampled. Probability sampling is essential if we wish to ensure that our sample is representative of the population. However, there are several different types of probability sampling, but something that underpins them all is the concept of randomness.

Remember when we were talking about different experimental designs and one of the key things in between-subject designs was random allocation to groups? The goal of this was to ensure that participant characteristics are evenly distributed across experimental conditions, thus ensuring

> **Random sampling**. Sampling where every member of the population of interest has an equal probability of being selected to take part in a study.

effects found are due to experimental manipulation and not preexisting differences between participants in each group. Randomness is also essential to sampling; we use it to ensure that we are not collecting people based on specific characteristics driven by the sampling method used e.g. a small set of people who log on to a specific webpage advertising experiments at the Lancaster University.

Simple Random Sampling

In simple random sampling, every member of the population of interest has an equal probability of being selected to take part in a study. This is often done using computer-generated random numbers.

Everyone in the population is given a code and then the computer randomly selects people to take part. This random selection ensures that your sample is representative of your population. It is notable that the bigger the sample you take the more likely it is to match the population. Another important thing is that you shouldn't try and generate random numbers yourself, i.e. just write down what you think a random numbers, as they won't be true random numbers – people are rubbish at being random (despite what contestants on Love Island say about themselves).

Let's look at some of our past examples and consider random sampling:

1 Fear of childbirth is going to be associated with postpartum anxiety

Let's say I am only interested in a local population so my population of interest is going to be pregnant people under the care of Liverpool Women's Hospital. So to be a random sample every currently pregnant person under the care of Liverpool Women's Hospital would need to have an equal chance of taking part because I am going to randomly choose 100 of them to take part. Now my population could be broader (e.g. all of the UK), or narrower (pregnant people under the care of Liverpool Women's Hospital who are between 7 and 8 months pregnant). Regardless of how wide or narrow the population of interest, what matters is the people within it have an equal chance of being selected.

2 "Consuming alcohol would result in more errors on a driving simulator".

The population of interest here are drivers who consume alcohol (not at the same time!). This is a really hard population to sample randomly. The first bit is easier I could get information from the DVLA, but how would I know if they consume alcohol? Things are challenging here as I cannot do a random sample of that population. Even if I narrow the population down to people in Merseyside who drive and consume alcohol. It's still really challenging to do. I could build a database of people who drive and consume alcohol and then randomly sample that (although this is impractical, and the database may not match the population). This shows that sometimes random sampling is really difficult.

Although random sampling is ideal in reality, especially when dealing with large populations of interest, it is often impossible to do!

Systematic random sampling

A systematic random sample is very similar to random sampling, except we only need to randomly select one number, which is our starting point. Following this, we recruit every nth participant in our population list (e.g.

every 10th person in the list). Imagine we have a population of people currently pregnant and under the care of Liverpool Women's Hospital, and there are 500 of them. I could randomly generate a number between one and ten as my starting point, then recruit every tenth person. This would give me a sample of 50 and everyone would have had an equal chance of being selected to take part from the outset (before the random number was selected).

Stratified sampling

Stratified sampling is quite a departure from random sampling although is still a form of probability sampling. It is particularly useful when you want to take a small sample. To do this you need to have a detailed understanding of your population and the strata that exist within it.

Stratified sampling. Where the population is divided into distinct subgroups based on specific characteristics, which are then randomly sampled from.

Essentially what you do is break down your population on factors, for example in our population of pregnant people under the care of Liverpool Women's Hospital we may know that for 30% of them, it's the first child, 40% their second child, 20% their third child and 10% their fourth or more child. So you may choose this as a strata. If I want to recruit 50 people, I would recruit like this:

Table 10.1 Stratified sampling for recruiting 50 participants

Children	% in population	Number recruited
1st child	30	15
2nd child	40	20
3rd child	20	10
4th or more child	10	5

It is, however, essential that you **randomise picks from within these strata**, where it is their first child all members of that group have an equal chance of being picked, and so on. Of course, we can have multiple strata and strata within strata. For example, we may want to stratify by whether they are a high-risk pregnancy. We would need to know the population stats for high-risk pregnancies. Let's say it's 20% high risk and 80% low risk. We would need to recruit accordingly. But there's a chance that these strata differ within groups which is what happens in the below example in Table 10.1.

If you were randomly sampling from the number of children strata, you would hope that this would ensure that you get a representative number of high-risk and low-risk pregnancies; but in this case where the sample is small then you can see how you could easily fail to recruit any high-risk pregnancies, particularly in the last two groups.

Stratified sampling can have some key advantages, firstly like random sampling it is a form of probability sampling meaning that your sample will be representative. It is also good if you have rare subgroups that could be missed out by random sampling as in stratified sampling you target them directly. Indeed we want to be inclusive in our sampling to avoid missing out on subgroups (see Chapter 17).

However, you need to have a good understanding of your population if you are going to stratify your sample, if you simply don't know how many high and low-risk pregnancies there are you cannot stratify by it. You also must make sure that the strata cover everyone in your population, if it does not then it is not probability sampling as some people may not be in a strata. This is why in the number of children strata in the example above I have the final group as 4th or more child. If I didn't do that and kept specific numbers, e.g. 4th child, 5th child, 6th child then someone may not be in my strata (see Table 10.2).

Table 10.2 Stratified sampling for recruiting 50 participants

Children	% in population	% High Risk low/risk within strata	Number recruited
1st child	30	20	3
		80	12
2nd child	40	40	16
		60	24
3rd child	20	10	2
		90	18
4th or more child	10	10	1
		90	9

Table 10.3 Bad stratification

Children	% in population
1st child	30
2nd child	40
3rd child	20
4th child	5
5th child	2
6th child	1

% in population column adds up to 98%, there's 2% of the population having their 7th or more child. These have a 0% probability of being picked in this stratification

Cluster sampling

Cluster sampling is a probability sampling technique in which you randomly sample clusters of individuals rather than the individuals.

> **Cluster sampling.** where clusters of individuals are randomly sampled.

We can use the "Superphonics" example to see how this could be done. My population here is children in their first year of school aged between 4-and 5 years old, and let's say for simplicity's sake my population of interest is children in Torfaen County Borough Council (*Cyngor Bwrdeistref Sirol Torfaen*) schools. There are 25 schools in the local authority and there are three classes in each year of these schools with 30 children in them.

For my Superphonics experiment, I want to have two groups of thirty. Instead of randomly sampling individuals across the 25 schools, which is unworkable as I would have to take children out of different schools and get them together in a classroom to teach them "Superphonics" or do a control lesson. Instead, I can cluster sample in which I randomly sample two classes, from the 75 classes (25 schools x 3 classes per year) and then randomly assign one of my classes to the Superphonics condition and one to the control condition.

This is not an ideal method of sampling as the clusters may not be that representative of the population. Some schools may be much better than others leaving us with unbalanced groups.

Non-Probability sampling

Sometimes, or to be honest often, it is not possible to use probability sampling techniques and we have to rely on non-probability sampling techniques instead. **Essentially, in**

> **Non-probability sampling.** Where not every individual has a known or equal chance of being included.

non-probability sampling not every individual has a known or equal chance of being included. We use these methods when it's difficult or impractical to use probability sampling.

Non-probability sampling is generally more convenient and far cheaper to do. Indeed, as an undergraduate student when you do research I think it is likely that you will be doing non-probability sampling. If you use non-probability sampling your work will come with a limitation, you will not be able to generalise your results to your population with a known level of accuracy.

Opportunity sample (aka convenience sample)

This is where you recruit people who meet your inclusion criteria but otherwise, you are recruiting anyone who agrees to do your study. For example, you may advertise your study on social media, the people who follow your accounts will be those who are going to

> **Opportunity sample (aka convenience sample).** Where the sample consists of anyone willing and eligible to do your study.

take part. Maybe at your university, there is an experiment participation scheme in which first years have to take part in studies. This would be another example of an opportunity sample. Indeed, participants being undergraduate students is a big problem in psychology research and something discussed in Chapter 17.

This is what non-probability sampling could look like in our example studies:

- In my Superphonics example, it may be I have contacts in a single school and then only two teachers agree for me to run my experiment in their classes. This would be an opportunity sample as I am taking the classes I can get, there is no avenue for randomisation of my sample.
- Maybe for my postpartum anxiety and fear of childbirth study I hand out flyers in antenatal classes to recruit. This would be opportunity sampling I'm only getting to the pregnant people who are attending classes on the day I give out flyers. I can try and go to areas with different demographics to improve the representativeness of the sample but it would still not be probability sampling.
- For my alcohol and driving simulator errors experiment I may recruit undergrad students who are in my University as it will be convenient for them to attend testing sessions and save me a considerable amount of time and money recruiting.

When doing this sort of sampling, you can collect some sample data from your participants and see how they match the population. In the latter example above, it may be my sample is quite young, this would be a limitation in the research and something future research could address.

This method often includes snowball sampling in which participants get other people they know to take part in a study. This is often done for harder-to-reach groups. This builds up samples but can be problematic, particularly in any study that involves manipulation or deceiving participants in some way as people may reveal what goes on in the experiment to their friends.

Haphazard sampling

In this method, the researcher will approach people to take part without any sort of structured approach or underlying randomisation process. They will select the sample based on convenience, ease of access, or spur-of-the-moment decisions, rather than following a systematic method. For example for my alcohol driving simulator study I could walk into the library and approach people "at random" (it's not random though as we don't have randomisers in our head) and ask them to take part. Of course, you probably would not be doing this completely randomly, for example, are you going to approach someone quietly humming to themselves while cleaning their feet with some sort of toe knife?

> **Haphazard sampling.** A technique where the research recruits without any sort of structured approach or underlying randomisation process.

Quota sampling

Here, the population is segmented into mutually exclusive sub-groups, like in stratified sampling *but* sampling from within these groups is not random (like it is in stratified). Instead, it is opportunity sampling. This is common in market research. People on high streets will ask you because they believe you fit a criteria (e.g. less than 30, female), but you have not been randomly sampled. You are approached because you are walking past them when they need to fill the quota. Once the quota is full they will not be interested in someone in your subgroup.

> **Quota sampling.** Where the population is segmented into mutually exclusive sub-groups, but sampling from within these groups is not random.

Maybe when doing the alcohol and driving simulator study I want 50% males and 50% females. Once I have recruited all the males I need I would focus on recruiting females. Again the key thing here is that within the subgroups/strata, I would not be randomly sampling.

Sample size

You have a method to take your sample, but how many participants are you going to recruit?

Remember the discussion in the last chapter about p values? One of their properties is that they are influenced by sample size. The bigger the sample, the smaller the p-value is going to be. So you want to have a sample size that will be big enough to adequately test your hypothesis. If your sample size is very small, then you are unlikely to find a statistically significant effect even if one exists (a false negative, or type 2 error). However, if your sample size is massive then trivially small effects will give you significant p-values, which may be pretty meaningless.

The best way to determine the sample size that you need is to do what is called a power calculation, specifically an *a priori* power calculation. In power calculations you need to know:

- α: the critical level of p (usually set to p<.05); which is the probability of rejecting a true null hypothesis (false positive aka type 1 error)
- β: the probability of failing to reject a false null hypothesis (false negative, aka type two error), this is usually set to .2 or .1
- the expected effect size/effect size of interest,
- The design of your study, different designs need different calculations

β is often set to .2 as the researcher is accepting a 20% chance of committing a type 2 error; this is commonly known as 80% power (100%-20%=80%). This value is a pragmatic trade-off, as it gives a reasonable chance of detecting a true effect without having to get a very large sample. It is, however, worth noting that many clinical trials have 90% power.

Power can be complicated and the psychological literature is littered with incorrect power calculations with them being more likely to be incorrect the more complex the analyses get!

Again, there is often a pragmatic approach that needs to be taken. Often the answer to questions about sample size is "as many as you can get". Some people argue that big samples are problematic due to the producing loads of significant effects. I don't have a problem with this, as I don't just rely on p values! By reporting effect sizes and confidence intervals with my work I am using the full tool kit of stats, meaning that I can report a significant p-value and tell the reader that the effect size is small so the finding may not be particularly important.

If you end up with a small sample, you are unlikely to find a significant effect when analysing your data, but again, you can report the effect size. Furthermore, if you do have a small sample size and have a significant effect it's really worth checking that this significant effect is not driven by an outlier (someone with a particularly high or low value on a variable that makes them very different from the rest of the sample).

Let's look at the power issues through the lens of the Superphonics experiment, in this I have a dependent variable that is a score on a test out of 20.

- In Table 10.4 I have only five students in each group and find no significant effect of the intervention even though it worked pretty well with scores being on average 4.4 higher in the Superphonics group.

Table 10.4 Five participants in each Superphonics condition

Superphonics score /20	Superphonics score /20
17	15
18	15
18	11
17	15
12	8

- If, however, I got lucky and recruited 1000 children in each condition (data not shown!) even a tiny difference between groups (control mean 12.2, Superphonics mean 12.5) would be statistically significant.

The lack of power in the first instance means that I don't think my intervention is effective. In the other one, the big sample means I think it is. So, as you can see, power matters!

Conclusion

Sampling is a critical part of quantitative research. In an ideal world, we use probability sampling to ensure our sample represents our population of interest, with randomness playing a key role in this. However, sometimes we cannot do random sampling and we have to sample what we can get, if this is the case you have a limitation that you need to be upfront about. Remember though when critically evaluating others' work; you can look at how they did their sampling, and check if their sample is representative.

Further Reading

Som, R. K. (1995). *Practical sampling techniques.* CRC press.
Emerson, R. W. (2015). Convenience sampling, random sampling, and snowball sampling: How does sampling affect the validity of research?. *Journal of visual impairment & blindness*, 109(2), 164–168.

Chapter 11

Testing associations

Introduction

This chapter will begin with a simple description of linear models and how they underpin much statistical analysis. It will then progress to discuss simple correlational analyses and the appropriate application of common forms of correlation (Pearson's and Spearman's) and how the former is poorly suited to testing non-linear relationships. Next, the fundamentals of linear regression (explained variance vs. unexplained variance) will be shown in simple diagrammatic terms to help the reader through this concept that underpins many analyses in this and, indeed, the subsequent chapter. This section will discuss regression coefficients and their interpretation (in both standardised and unstandardised formats). Model assumptions will be discussed as well.

Finally, there will be a brief discussion of generalised linear models and how they are applied according to the way a study measures its dependent variable. Logistic regression will get some expanded discussion inasmuch as maximum likelihood models along with odds ratios and their meaning. Other generalised linear models will be briefly discussed.

Correlational research

In Chapter 7 we discussed correlational research where researchers want to examine the association between two or more variables. These designs enable us to understand the direction of the relationships between variables and the strength of the relationship between variables.

Unlike experimental research, there is no manipulation of variables at all; we simply collect data and then identify associations. This chapter is going to look at how we statistically test these associations.

DOI: 10.4324/9781032656564-14

A quick point on linear models

We are now into statistics! In the opening chapter, I acknowledged you probably didn't start to do a degree in Psychology because you wanted to do statistics but it is incredibly important to the subject and there are only a few core concepts that you need to know to be able to understand statistics. One of these things is that, despite having different names (and being used in different study designs), most common statistical methods we use are a form of linear model. We are creating linear models to be able to predict our DV from our IV(s). These linear models all boil down to one concept, the formula:

$$y = bX + a$$

Y = thing we are predicting (the dependent variable value)
b = slope of the line
X = value of the predictor
a = intercept (where the line crosses the Y-axis)

This can be shown graphically in Figure 11.1 where we have the slope (line of best fit; more on this in a moment) and we have an intercept based on where the slope crosses the X-axis.

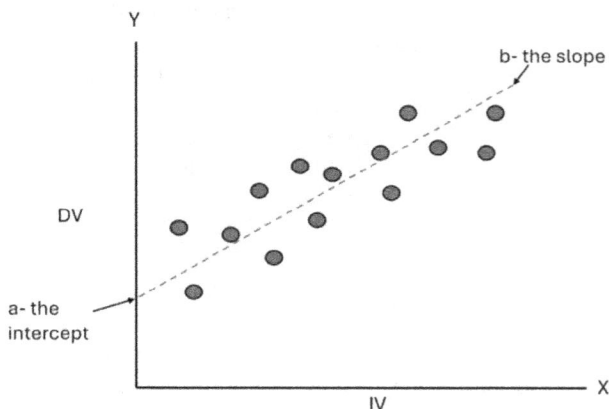

Figure 11.1 Linear model showing the intercept (a) and the slope (b)

Based on this, I can predict the value of the DV based on a known value of the IV. In Figure 11.2 you can see how we can make a prediction from this line, if someone has a value of 3 on the IV the DV value is predicted to be about 48, whereas if someone has a value of 8 on the IV their predicted value of the DV will be 80.

Much of what I discuss in the next chapter is also a linear model (which I will demonstrate). Indeed, there is a fantastic blog post by Jonas Kristoffer Lindeløv (Lindeløv 2019), that breaks all this down, it is quite advanced so I wouldn't rush to read it right now but in the future, once you have a good grasp of statistics it may be something you wish to read. But the key thing is with the tests of association we are dealing with here they are ultimately forms of linear models, different calculations underpin them, but they are all ultimately about making predictions and are looking at the strength of associations between variables.

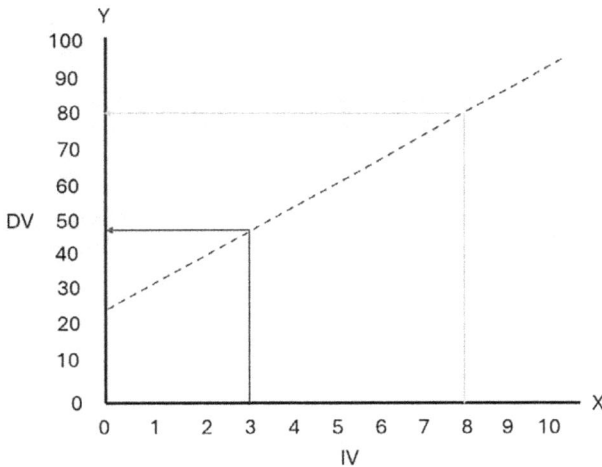

Figure 11.2 Making predictions based on linear models.

Associations

When looking at associations there are two things we need to consider, the direction of an association and the strength of association. Let's look at the correlational study we discussed before, the association between postpartum anxiety and fear of childbirth.

We would likely expect there to be a positive association between postpartum anxiety and fear of childbirth (A in Figure 11.3). This means that people with high anxiety are also more likely to have a greater fear of childbirth. However, there may be an unexpected negative association between postpartum anxiety and fear of childbirth (B in Figure 11.3). This means that those with high postpartum anxiety will have less fear of childbirth. When we talk about associations we must talk about whether it is a positive or negative association, hopefully, it's obvious why that matters! We could have no association at all between these two variables; this would look like C in Figure 11.3.

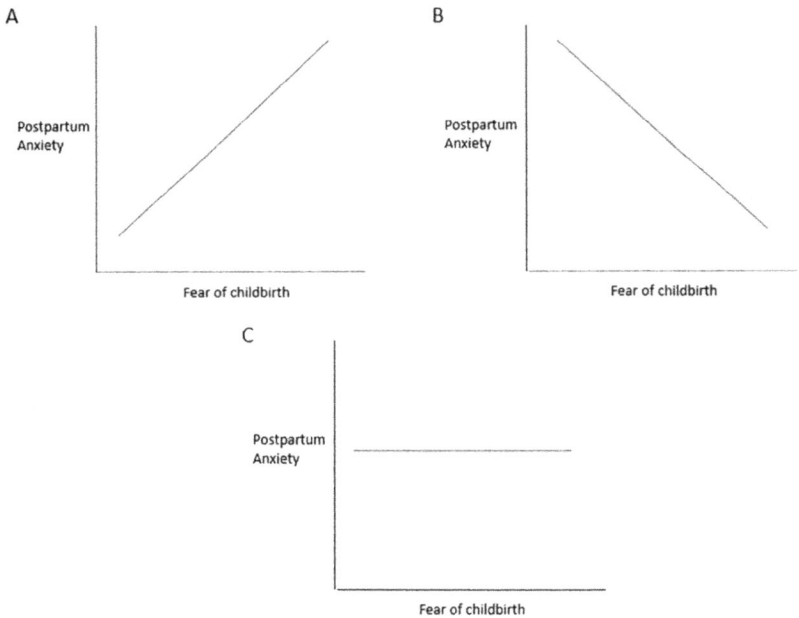

Figure 11.3: A positive (A), negative (B) and no association (C) between postpartum anxiety and fear of childbirth

However, this is not all that we are interested in, we also need to consider the strength of the association between variables. We may have a clear positive association between variables but it may be very weak. This can be demonstrated in Figure 11.4. In A there is a very strong association; any prediction we make from this would be accurate. In B there is a weak association, and any predictions made from this would be inaccurate. The slope is the same but the association is weak in one and not the other.

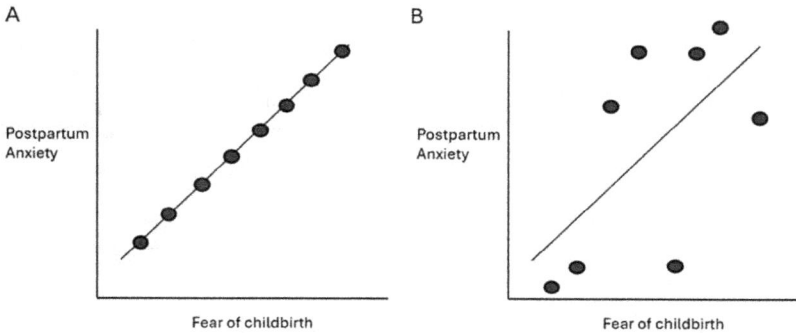

Figure 11.4 Strong (A) vs. Weak (B) associations

Testing associations: Correlations

The simplest way of looking at associations between two variables is by correlating them. **There are two forms of correlations, parametric (typically Pearson's correlation) and non-parametric (typically Spearman's correlation).** You may remember the inventors of these methods Pearson and Spearman from Chapter 2.

> **Pearson's correlation.** A parametric statistical test that tests the association between two variables.

Parametric statistical tests make assumptions about data to be valid. Parametric correlations assume:

- There is a linear association between the two variables
- Data are interval or ratio
- Data should have an approximate normal distribution (slight deviations don't matter)
- It is often argued that there should be no big outliers, although the importance of this in big samples, or if the outliers follow a linear association, is debatable.

> **Non-parametric test.** A test that doesn't make specific assumptions about data.

> **Spearman's correlation.** A non-parametric statistical test that tests the association between two variables.

When I say the assumption of a linear association I mean A in Figure 11.5, as values of Fear of childbirth go up, postpartum anxiety also goes up in a consistent manner. In B in Figure 11.5 this is not the case, at first, there is little association between fear of childbirth and postpartum anxiety but halfway along the X axis (the horizontal one) there is a big positive association between fear of childbirth and postpartum anxiety.

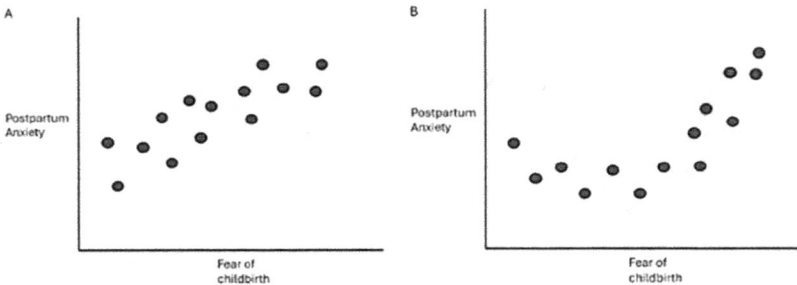

Figure 11.5 A linear and non-linear association
Note: A is sometimes called a monotonic association and B is non-monotonic

In the case of B, a parametric correlation (e.g. Pearson's) is going to be less effective, instead, a non-parametric test would need to be used (e.g. Spearman's). These non-parametric correlations do not make assumptions about the data (except that the data is *not* nominal).

> **Parametric statistical test**. A test that makes specific assumptions about data.

Pearson's correlation

Pearson's correlation uses the following formula.

$$ r = \frac{\Sigma(x_i - \bar{x})(y_i - \bar{y})}{\sqrt{\Sigma(x_i - \bar{x})^2 \Sigma y^2 - (\Sigma y_i - \bar{y})^2}} $$

r = The correlation coefficient – our test statistic
x_i = values on the x variable
y_i = values on the y variable
$\bar{x}$ = mean of x
$\bar{y}$ = mean of y

> **Correlation coefficient.** A metric of association, ranging between -1 and 1.

The key thing is that it uses the raw scores from the data set, and to do this it makes assumptions about the data, like the numbers having a real meaning (i.e. interval or ratio data), and not being abstract (ordinal data). However, because it uses raw data it is really poor at identifying non-linear effects and if the data set is small it can be influenced by extreme values.

You will probably run Pearson's correlations in your degree using some form of software (you may also do it by hand). When you run correlations you will get three pieces of information out of it:

r = The correlation coefficient

- **A correlation coefficient is a metric of association.** It ranges between -1 "perfect negative association" and 1 "perfect positive association". With 0 meaning no association at all. Pearson's r is also an effect size, so we can judge how strong our association is by its value with .1 being small, .3 being medium and. 6 being large.

df= the degrees of freedom

- The degrees of freedom are N (number of participants) -2. All parametric tests have degrees of freedom and they are calculated differently depending on the test. **They represent the number of values that are free to vary when producing the test statistic.** The degrees of freedom in conjunction with the r value is what produces the p value. The larger the degrees of freedom the more likely a fixed r value is to be significant as they effectively represent the sample size (and remember that p values are based on, in part sample size).

> **Df (degrees of freedom).** the number of values that are free to vary when producing the test statistic.

P= the p-value for the association.

- See Chapter 9.

The correlation is written up in a specific manner, let's pretend we got 60 people to complete our postpartum anxiety fear of childbirth study and found a positive association between the two measures. This would be written up as:

"There was a significant positive association between fear of childbirth and postpartum anxiety (r(58)=.31, p=.013."

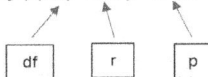

| df | r | p |

Spearman's correlation (sometimes called Spearman's rank correlation)

This uses the formula if their are tied ranks (i.e. some scores are identical – often the case!):

$$r_s = 1 - \frac{6\Sigma d^2}{n(n^2 - 1)}$$

r_s = The correlation coefficient
d = the difference between the *ranks* of the pairs of observations
n = number of observations (often the number of participants)

The fundamental difference here is that this formula doesn't use the raw data, it uses the ranks of the data. Essentially each of the two variables is put into rank order (from lowest value to highest value) and then a rank is assigned to each variable. For example, fear of childbirth is measured using a slider in which participants state how much fear of childbirth they have from 1 (none) to 100 (terrified). I have 11 participants who did this and then I have put them in rank order.

Table 11.1 Values for variable Fear of childbirth and the difference between each successive value

Fear of childbirth	Difference from the previous value
1	-
4	3
5	1
6	1
7	1
9	2
12	2
13	1
15	2
39	24
60	21

I have some big outliers here and the data set is small. This may influence my results if a parametrc test is used.

If I rank Fear of childbirth then:

Table 11.2 Ranking fear of childbirth and showing the difference between these ranks

Fear of childbirth	Difference from the previous value	Rank	Difference (rank)
1	-	1	-
4	3	2	1
5	1	3	1
6	1	4	1
7	1	5	1
9	2	6	1
12	2	7	1
13	1	8	1
15	2	9	1
39	24	10	1
100	61	11	1

> The difference shown here is not the same as d in the formula above (which is the difference between ranks of the two variables being correlated) I'm just illustrating why ranks have an influence on the data.

The rank difference (4th column) is completely consistent as the ranking has converted the raw data. Therefore the high values of fear of childbirth (last two rows) are no longer high values, so when we do our calculation to get a correlation coefficient these will not have an undue influence on results.

This ranking is also suitable for ordinal data. Moreover, ranking enables the identification of some non-linear associations like curvilinear monotonic relationships (which is what Figure 11.5 B is). In this figure, as one variable increases the other also increases but in a non-linear manner, producing a nonlinear positive association. A Pearson's correlation in this case would say there is a weaker association than a Spearman's correlation would.

Let's say we take our fear of childbirth on our 1–100 ordinal scale and measure postpartum anxiety on a 1–5 scale ranging from (not anxiety – 1 to severe anxiety – 5) in 40 participants. This gives two ordinal outcomes so we need to do a Spearman's correlation. This is written up in an almost identical manner to Pearson's except instead of r we report r_s (so our reader knows it's a Spearman's correlation). In this I find a significant association, it would be written up as:

"There was a significant positive association between fear of childbirth and postpartum anxiety ($r_s(38)=.49$, p=.001."

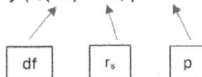

df r_s p

Beyond correlation to Linear regression

In a linear regression, we are looking at associations between one or more IVs (predictors) and a ratio or interval DV (people often use ordinal DVs but they shouldn't! – If you

> **Linear regression.** A test that explores associations between one or more IVs (predictors) and a ratio or interval DV.

find a paper that does this that's a critical appraisal point!). In a linear regression, we are putting in our line of best fit.

The line of best fit is the line between each pair of observations that has the lowest squared differences.

This gives us what is called the sum of squared errors. This is how inaccurate the line of best fit is. The formula is:

$$SSE = \sum\nolimits_{i=1}^{n} (y_i - \hat{y})^2$$

y_i = *an observation*
$\hat{y}$ = *a prediction*
$\bar{y}$ = *mean*

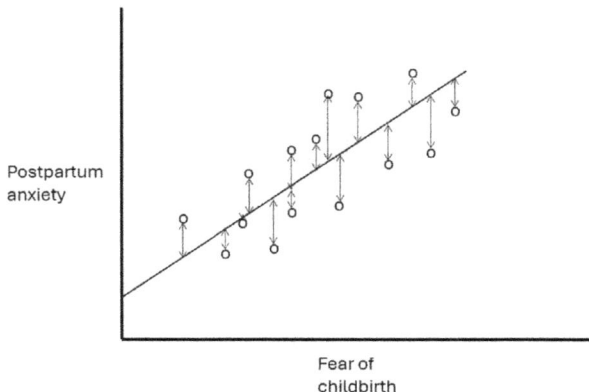

Postpartum anxiety

Fear of childbirth

Figure 11.6 Line of best fit

So that's how much variance our predictor(s) is unable to explain. But what of the variance it does explain? That is calculated through the sum of the squared difference between the mean and the predicted value for each observation (known as the sum of squares model, SSM; see figure 11.7).

There are only two types of variance, variance we can explain, and variance we cannot explain. So if we add up SSM and SSE we get SST (total variance).

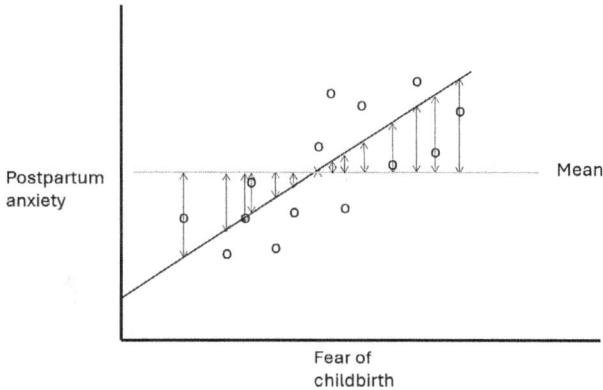

Figure 11.7 Variance in the DV explained (SSM)

This enables us to do something clever: if we divide the SSM (variance explained) by SST (total variance) this will tell us the **proportion of variance our regression model explained!** This statistic is known as R^2:

$$R^2 = \frac{SSM}{SSM + SSE} = \frac{SSM}{SST}$$

R^2 can range between 0 and 1, 0 being no variance is explained, 1 being all the variance is explained by the predictor(s) so it's easy to interpret:

- R^2 =.5 means 50% of variance is accounted for
- R^2 =.02 means 2% of variance is accounted for

There is also a version of it called Adjusted R^2. This punishes the R^2 statistic for every IV added, this stops people from adding variables in an attempt to produce a good model. Essentially if you add an IV that doesn't predict much variance R^2 will stay the same or go up a little bit, however, adjusted R^2 will go down, indeed it is possible to get a negative adjusted R^2.

R^2. The proportion of variance a regression model explains.

We also test if our overall regression is statistically significant. This is done with an F statistic (more on these in the next chapter). This is the mean squares for the model (MSM) divided by the mean squared error MSE.

$$F = \frac{MSM}{MSE}$$

The F statistic comes with the degrees of freedom which are (K, N-K-1) where K is the number of predictors in the model and N is the number of participants in the sample. The F-statistic and dfs are then used to calculate the p-value, i.e. is the proportion of variance explained (given the number of predictors and the sample size) significant?

Let's imagine I did correlational research predicting postpartum anxiety, but I have four predictors (fear of childbirth, age, number of previous children, current level of stress) and I have 230 participants. I will get a single R^2, F and p-value for this model, this will tell me the extent to which these variables predict postpartum anxiety. This would be written up like this:

The model was significant adjusted R^2=.07, F(4,225)=4.96, p<.001

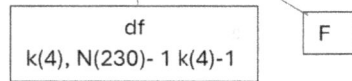

df	F
k(4), N(230)- 1 k(4)-1	

If R^2 as opposed to Adjusted R^2 was reported it wouldn't make a difference to the other statistics.

But what about the individual predictors we put in our model? We only know that taken together, our predictors account for a significant amount of variance. We also need to look at individual predictors in the model using regression coefficients.

Regression coefficients

We need to know if there is an association between each of the IVs (predictors) in our model and the DV (outcome), and also the direction the association is (positive or negative). A regression coefficient (B) helps us to understand this.

> **Regression coefficient.** The association between each predictor and outcome (in terms of unit changes).

I love regression coefficients because they are not abstract at all: they can be **interpreted as for a one-unit change in the IV, this is how much the DV changes.**

In our previous example, we had the number of previous children as an IV. If we got a regression coefficient of -1 this would mean for each previous child (i.e. as the IV goes up by one) postpartum anxiety scores, go *down* by one. If:

- B= 0.5 for each previous child postpartum anxiety increases by 0.5 units
- B= 2.7 for each previous child postpartum anxiety increases by 2.7 units
- B= -0.50 for each previous child postpartum anxiety decreases by 0.5 units
- B= -3.12 for each previous child postpartum anxiety decreases by 3.12 units

However, regression coefficients also come with what is called a standard error (SE). This is on average how wrong each of our predictions is across all observations. It is also in terms of unit changes. A small SE means the regression coefficient estimation is more precise.

- SE = 0.5; the average distance our coefficient is from the observed value is. 5 units
- SE = 1.2; the average distance our coefficient is from the observed value is 1.2 units

We also get a p-value for the regression coefficients. The ratio of the regression coefficient to the standard error gives a t-statistic, and from this t-statistic a p-value is produced:

$$t = \frac{B}{SE}$$

This is often written up as:

There was a significant association between the number of previous children and postpartum anxiety (B= -1.30, SE=0.54, p=.016).

Confidence intervals are often reported with these as well, these refer to the regression coefficient, and would be just added to a write-up:

There was a significant association between the number of previous children and postpartum anxiety (B= -1.30, SE=0.54, p=.016, 95%CI= -2.36 to -0.24).

Standardised regression coefficients – Beta (β)

There are also standardised coefficients as well (and these don't have standard errors). They explain the associations between IVs (predictors) and DV (outcome) not in terms of units but in terms of standard deviation changes.

Standardised regression coefficients – Beta (β). The association between each predictor and outcome (in terms of standard deviation changes).

- β=1.50 means that for every 1 standard deviation increase in the IV, there is a 1.50 standard deviation *increase* in the DV
- β= -2.50 meaning for each standard deviation increase in the IV, there is a 2.50 standard deviation *decrease* in the DV.

I don't like these because I don't like to think in terms of standard deviations because NO ONE THINKS LIKE THIS! However, they do have a use. Because they are standardised in terms of standard deviations, we can compare beta values and the biggest one is the strongest predictor. We can't do this with normal regression coefficients because they need to be considered with their standard errors. Beta values have the same p-value as a normal regression coefficient (it's the same information just expressed in terms of standard deviations).

Notably, not every outcome we want to predict is interval or ratio, and we may need to do other types of regression to analyse these.

Other regressions for testing associations

Here are some other regressions used to test associations.

Logistic regression

Sometimes we want to predict if someone falls into one of two groups e.g. clinically depressed vs. not clinically depressed. We cannot use a linear model on this as the outcome is categorical.

> **Logistic regression.** A test that explores associations between one or more IVs (predictors) and a two-level categorical DV.

Instead, we use a logistic regression, often called a binary logistic regression because the outcome is stated in binary terms (0 vs. 1). The big difference between linear and logistic regressions is that the latter is about likelihoods (e.g. the likelihood of being clinically depressed) rather than making predictions (like linear regression). However, much of the terminology is the same. Logistic models are all about predicting what group people will be in based on the IVs.

Model fit

Logistic regression doesn't produce an R^2 statistic. However, people who clearly like the sound of their own names, developed what are called pseudo-R^2 statistics (Nagelkerke R^2, Cox and Snell R^2, or McFadden R^2). They can be very inconsistent with each other though. I also think they encourage people to conflate linear models with logistic models so I don't like them much. However, logistic regressions produce a correct classification rate (usually as a %). This is the percentage of participants the model classified as being in the correct group of the DV. We also get a p-value for this, although it is based on a Chi-squared (X^2) test statistic and not an F-statistic.

Regression coefficients

Like linear regression (and indeed all regressions!), logistic regression will give you regression coefficients and standard errors. However, instead of being interpreted as the number of unit changes in the DV for each 1 unit change in the IV, they are the change in the *log-odds* of being in the group labelled 1 (remember the outcome groups are labelled 0 or 1) for each one unit change in the IV. For example, imagine we use fear of childbirth (IV) to predict a diagnosis of postpartum anxiety (DV; 0 no postpartum anxiety, 1 postpartum anxiety), and we get a regression coefficient of 0.8. This means that, for every unit increase in fear of childbirth, the log odds of being diagnosed with postpartum anxiety increase by 0.8. Like linear regression (1), we get a standard error that is essentially the variability in the regression coefficient across each participant, and (2) the coefficient divided by the SE gives a critical ratio (Z rather than t in logistic regression) which we use to produce the p-value for the individual association.

Jaccard (2001) describes log odds as difficult to interpret and a detailed explanation is not appropriate for an introductory social science textbook. It is also a bit unnecessary as we more often than not exponentialize the regression coefficient to produce what is called an odds ratio (OR). An odds ratio shows the change in odds of being in the category labelled 1 that results from a one-unit change in the IV.

$$OR = \frac{Odds\ after\ a\ unit\ change\ in\ the\ IV}{Original\ odds}$$

ORs are easier to interpret; again let's use fear of childbirth (IV) to predict the likelihood of a postpartum anxiety diagnosis (0 = no postpartum anxiety, 1 = postpartum anxiety). OR=1 means no change as the IV increases; values above 1 mean that as the IV increases the likelihood of having a postpartum anxiety diagnosis increases; values below one mean the likelihood of having a postpartum anxiety diagnosis decrease. Let's look at some examples:

OR of 1 = unit change in fear of childbirth is associated with no change in the likelihood of postpartum anxiety.

OR of 1.5 = unit change in fear of childbirth is associated with a 50% increase in the likelihood of postpartum anxiety.

OR of 4.7 = unit change in fear of childbirth is associated with a 370% increase in the likelihood of postpartum anxiety.

OR of 0.5 = unit change in fear of childbirth is associated with a 50% decrease in the likelihood of postpartum anxiety.

OR of 0.514 = unit change in fear of childbirth is associated with a 48.6% decrease in the likelihood of postpartum anxiety.

Poisson regression

Poisson regression is used when your dependent variable is a count (e.g. number of times arrested, number of relapses, number of bankruptcies). So we have independent events over a (fixed) period.

Ordinal regression

A big bugbear of mine is that people take ordinal outcomes and use them in linear regression models. I think you should be using ordinal regressions instead.

Multinomial regression

Multinomial regression is like a logistic regression but for when your DV has three or more categories. The categories in these regressions cannot be put into a logical order (so you cannot use an ordinal model in this case).

In these three regressions, model fit is tested (through a Chi Square statistic,) pseudo R^2 values are produced, and regression coefficients with standard errors are produced (although interpretation differs).

Conclusion

We have now covered numerous ways of testing associations. The key thing to remember is that you need to choose the correct method based on the properties of your data. If you select a method that is not suitable for your data, you cannot trust your results! Correlations are the simplest measures of association but we can look at more complicated models with regressions. Fortunately, regressions (although the calculations underpinning them differ) follow the same general rules, model fit statistics tell you if your overall model predicts the DV, and then regression coefficients show you individual associations between IVs and the DV Although they all produce regression coefficients these are interpreted differently depending on the model type. In the next chapter, we will look at testing differences between groups rather than associations, although the underpinning of many of these tests is linear regression.

Further Reading

See my (Professor Paul Christiansen) Youtube channel for video guides in data analysis covering three different software (SPSS, R and JASP) https://www.youtube.com/channel/UCpjsdW-snzkUAx0lvqTJ7WA.

Field, A. (2024). *Discovering statistics using IBM SPSS statistics / R.* Sage publications limited.

Lindeløv, J. K. (2019). Common statistical tests are linear models (or: How to teach stats).

References

Jaccard, J. (2001) *Interaction Effects in Logistic Regression*, Issue 135. SAGE.

Chapter 12

Data analysis – Comparing differences

Introduction

This chapter is going to focus on appropriate methods to analyse differences between conditions. First, we will cover analysing purely nominal data. Next, there will be a discussion of some simple tests of differences, covering one sample, within and between-subject designs with two conditions, before moving on to three+ conditions. The latter will come with a discussion of *post hoc* testing (which links back to Chapter 9). Throughout we will discuss the appropriateness of applying different analyses to different forms of data (i.e. parametric vs. nonparametric tests). Finally, there will be a discussion of multifactorial designs. For everything we cover, there will be examples of the statistics reported with these different tests.

Keeping it nominal

Sometimes you must analyse data that is purely nominal, that is, your variables consists of categories only. In some instances, you may simply have a single nominal variable and you want to know if some of the categories are more common than others. In Chapter 4 we covered an example of nominal data in which we asked people if they had different pets. For simplicity, let's imagine that there are only two types of pet people can have (and everyone has one). I ask 100 people what type of pet they have.

Table 12.1 Number of participants with each pet type (observed frequency)

Pet	Observed number
Dog	80
Cat	20

DOI: 10.4324/9781032656564-15

I may be interested if there is a significant difference in the frequency of different pets owned in my sample. This is done with a Chi-Square Goodness of fit test, which asks a simple question – is my observed data (i.e. what is in Table 12.1) different from what we would expect if all things were equal?

If all things were equal, what would I expect? I would expect 50 people to have dogs and 50 people to have cats (see Table 12.2).

> **Chi-Square Goodness of fit test.** A statistical test exploring frequencies in a single nominal variable.

This information and be used to calculate the Chi-square statistic and produce a p-value

$$\chi^2 = \Sigma \left[\frac{(O - E)^2}{E} \right]$$

E = expected value
O = observed value

For each observation you simply subtract the expected value from the observed value and then square it, finally dividing it by the expected value. You then add up these values to give the Chi-Square statistic (Table 12.3).

If we add up the final column, in Table 12.3 we get a chi-square (X^2) statistic (in this case 18+18=36). We also have a degree of freedom for this model, which is the number of categories we are testing -1 so df=1. We can then generate our p-value for our data using these two numbers. A chi-square statistic with one degree of freedom is significant (p<.05) if the statistic is greater than 3.84. So, we can say that significantly more people have a pet dog than a cat.

The write-up for the Chi-square goodness of fit tends to look like this:

Owning dogs was significantly more common than cats, $X^2(1)=36.00, p<.001$

| | df | X^2 | p |

Table 12.2 Number of participants with each pet type – observed and expected

Pet	Observed number	Expected number
Dog	80	50
Cat	20	50

Table 12.3 Calculating the Chi-square statistic

Pet	Observed number	Expected number	O – E	$(O – E)^2$	$(O – E)^2/E$
Dog	80	50	30	900	900/50 =18
Cat	20	50	-30	900	900/50 =18

An effect size can be reported to, this is usually Cramer's V which, according to Le Quéau et al. (2017), is interpreted as:

- V<0.1: very weak
- 0.1≤V<0.2: weak
- 0.2≤ V<0.3: medium
- ≥0.3: strong

We can take this a step further, perhaps we are interested in how dog and cat ownership differs across another nominal variable. This is analysed with

Chi-Square test of independence. A statistical test exploring frequencies across two nominal variables.

what is called a **Chi-Square test of independence.** For example, perhaps we are interested in dog and cat ownership among people who live in rural vs. urban areas. Our data may look like this:

Table 12.4 Number of participants with each pet type across rural and urban environments (observed frequency)

	Rural	*Urban*	*Total*
Dog	60	20	**80**
Cat	5	15	**20**
Total	**65**	**35**	**100**

We also have row totals (underlined) and column totals (bold) we use these to calculate expected frequencies. The following formula calculates the expected frequency for each cell:

$$\text{Expected frequencies} = \frac{\text{Observed frequency (row)} * \text{Observed Frequency (column)}}{N}$$

Table 12.5 Expected frequency for each pet type across rural and urban environments

	Rural	*Urban*
Dog	$\frac{80*65}{100} = 52$	$\frac{80*35}{100} = 28$
Cat	$\frac{20*65}{13} = 13$	$\frac{20*35}{100} = 7$

We then calculate the Chi-square statistic in the same way as before

Table 12.6 Calculating the Chi-square statistic

Pet/home	Observed number	Expected number	O – E	(O – E)²	(O – E)²/E
Dog/Rural	60	52	8	64	64/52 =1.23
Dog/Urban	20	28	-8	64	64/28 =2.29
Cat/Rural	5	13	-8	64	64/13=4.92
Cat/Urban	15	7	8	64	64/7=9.14

If we add up the final column, we get a chi-square (X^2) statistic: in this case it's 17.58. The degrees of freedom for this is calculated as:

$$df = (number\ of\ rows - 1) * (number\ of\ columns - 1)$$

In our case that will be (2–1) x (2–1) = 1. We use these two pieces of information to get a p-value. Statistical software will do this for you, in our case the p-value is p<.001. We write this up just like before, although describe it differently:

There was a significant difference in dog compared to cat ownership across rural and urban areas $X^2(1)=17.58, p<.001$.

When we are purely dealing with categorical data like this, we are almost certainly going to use a Chi-square test (unless we have a two-level categorical outcome as a DV and wish to have predictors of it then we use a logistic regression as described in Chapter 11).

Comparing groups with continuous outcomes

One sample t-tests (not actually comparing groups)

There may be a situation in which you wish to compare the scores of a single group to a fixed number. To illustrate this let's consider our alcohol and driving

> **One sample t-tests.** A statistical test to compare an interval/ratio dependent variable to fixed number.

error study. Perhaps we are interested in if the number of errors is significantly different from zero errors. In this case, we would have one group of 50 people, who have consumed alcohol and then complete the driving simulator.

We can use a one-sample t-test to explore this. It is a straightforward process (again you will use statistical software to do this for you) but the process is as follows.

1   We calculate the mean number of errors, I'll pretend that's 3.40.
2   Then we calculate the standard error of the mean; the variance divided by the square root of the sample size (I'll pretend that's 3 and 50 respectively):

$$\frac{s}{\sqrt{n}} = \frac{3}{\sqrt{50}} = 0.42$$

3   The mean is divided by the standard error to give the t statistic (the critical value):

$$t = \frac{3.40}{0.42} = 8.10$$

The degrees of freedom for this model are n-1 so in this case we have 50–1=49. The df along with the t statistic gives us a p-value, in this case, p<.001 (software will do this for us). We can write this up as:

Alcohol produced a statistically significant number of errors in the driving simulator t(49)=8.10, p<.001).

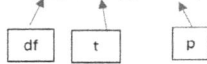

You can also produce Cohen's *d* effect size for this and indeed all t-tests; this gives you a magnitude of the difference (in this case between the sample mean and 0). Cohen's *d* interpretation:

Effect size	Use	Small	Medium	Large
Cohen's *d*	t-tests	0.2	0.5	0.8

Comparing two between-subject groups

When we have between-subjects designs, we need to compare different groups. The statistical test that we use will, however, depend on the statistical properties of the dependent variable. These properties will dictate to us whether we use a parametric or non-parametric statistical test.

Parametric test: Independent samples t-test

We can use this test when we meet some key assumptions.

> **Independent samples t-test.**
> A parametric test used to compare two, independent, groups.

- The data is interval or ratio.
- The data has an approximate normal distribution (this is not that important in a big sample).
- It also needs to show what is called homogeneity of variance.

Homogeneity of variance refers to the variance in the dependent variable being relatively even within the two groups. If one group has loads of variance and the other shows little variance then it will not meet this assumption.

> **Homogeneity of variance.** the assumption that variances in two or more between-subjects conditions/groups are relatively similar.

If you meet these assumptions an independent samples t-test can be run. This will tell you if the means of the two groups are significantly different. It can be viewed just like a regression (as covered in the previous chapter), although it looks a bit different when graphed.

We can use the Superphonics example here. We have the scores on the class test for the Superphonics and the control group. We want to see if they are significantly different from each other.

The formula tests how big the difference between the two means in comparison to pooled standard error, to put it simply:

$$t = \frac{x_1 - x_2}{standard\ error}$$

x_1 = mean in group 1
x_2 = mean in group 2

The bigger the mean difference compared to the standard error, the bigger your t statistic (the critical value), again this statistic along with the degrees of freedom (calculated as $(n_1 + n_2)$-2), with n meaning the number in each condition, produces us our p-value.

Imagine we have 10 children in each condition and find a significant difference between groups with better scores in Superphonics (mean=17.0) compared to the control condition (mean =13.2). We would write this up as:

Scores in the Superphonics condition were significantly higher than the control condition t(18)=3.05, p= .007.

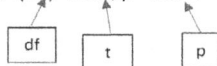

| df | t | p |

How is this like a regression then? In the figure below I have plotted the mean for each condition with the standard error, and drawn a line between the two means. This line is a line of best fit. I can continue this line to get an intercept (dotted). Individual data points are the dots.

Like with the one-sample t-test, we can also produce a Cohen's d effect size for this test.

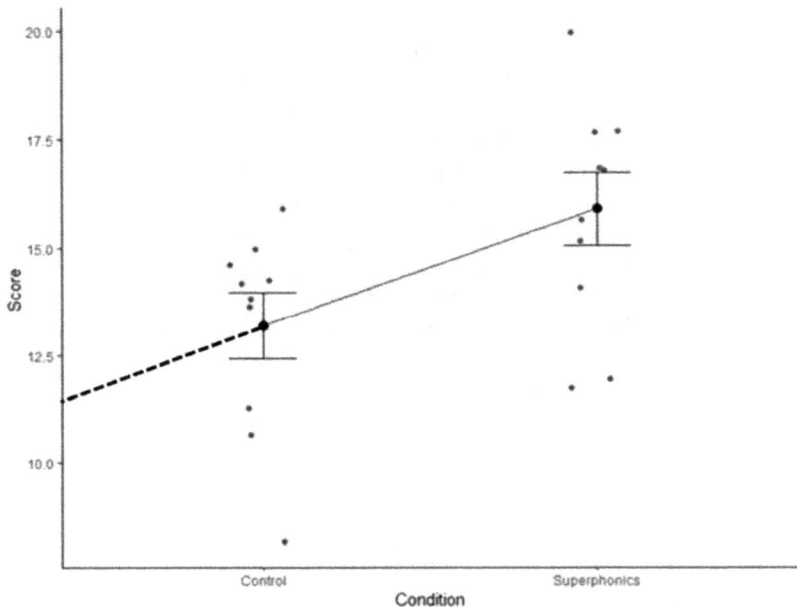

Figure 12.1 Thinking about regressions!

Welch test

One of the assumptions of the independent sample t-test is that you have homogeneity of variance. If this assumption is not met, then a Welch test can be conducted instead. It is written up in the same

> **Welch test**. A parametric test used to compare two, independent, groups when you do not have homogeneity of variance.

way as a standard t-test (the degree of freedom will almost inevitably have decimal places in it).

Mann-Whitney test (Wilcoxon rank-sum test)

This is the non-parametric test for comparing two between-subject groups. This doesn't make assumptions about the properties of the data; this means that is

> **Mann-Whitney test**. A non-parametric test used to compare two, independent, groups.

useful for ordinal data, smaller samples with non-normal distributions and/or big outliers. This is because this test converts the raw data into ranks. It ranks the data points from the two groups together. For example, let's say we did our Superphonics experiment and asked children to say how much they liked reading after the intervention using a child-friendly scale (1 meaning they hate it 5 they love it).

This scale is ordinal as we cannot be sure that children all interpret the responses the same (see Chapter 4).

Table 12.7 Our ordinal data

Superphonics	Control
3	2
4	3
5	2
2	4
4	2
1	1
3	3

It then ranks the data across groups, I'll reorder the raw data to make it clearer:

Table 12.8 Ordered data across groups

Superphonics	Control
1	
	1
2	
	2
	2
	2
3	
3	
	3
	3
4	
4	
	4
5	

We then assign a rank to the data.

Table 12.9 Ranking data across groups

Row	Superphonics	Control	Rank Superphonics	Rank Control
1	1		1.5	
2		1		1.5
3	2		4.5	
4		2		4.5
5		2		4.5
6		2		4.5
7	3		8.5	
8	3		8.5	
9		3		8.5
10		3		8.5
11	4		12	
12	4		12	
13		4		12
14	5		14	
			Total =61 (R_1)	Total =44 (R_2)

Note when ranks match, e.g. we have two number ones, we give the rank as the orders divided by the number of matches (1+2)/2. For another example, we have four 2's occupying rank space 3,4,5 and 6 so they are given the rank (3+4+5+6)/4.

We then calculate the test statistic which is called U. We do two of these, one for each condition:

$$U_1 = n_1 n_2 + \frac{n_1(n_1 + 1)}{2} - R_1$$
$$U_2 = n_1 n_2 + \frac{n_2(n_2 + 1)}{2} - R_2$$

In our data we would have:

Superphonics:

$$U_1 = 7x7 + \frac{7(7 + 1)}{2} - 61 = 16$$

Control:

$$U_1 = 7x7 + \frac{7(7 + 1)}{2} - 44 = 33$$

We take the smallest U as our critical value; in this case, U=16 so we have our critical value. This test doesn't have degrees of freedom but we judge the level of statistical significance based on the n in each condition, in this case 7 + 7. In this example our p value is non-significant. We can write this up as:

> There was no significant difference between the two conditions U= 16, N=14, p=.293.

There is a range of different effect sizes that we can give with a Mann-Whitney test, for example, Vargha and Delaney's A, Cliff's delta, or rank-biserial correlation coefficient (r).

Comparing two within-subject conditions

When we have two within-subject conditions we also have a choice of tests and again we need to use the appropriate test based on the properties of our data, with our choice being between a parametric or non-parametric test.

Parametric test: Paired samples t-test

We can use this test when we meet some key assumptions

Paired samples t-test. A para-metric test used to compare two, within-subjects, conditions.

- The data is interval or ratio
- The data has an approximate normal distribution (this is not that important in a big sample).

We will use the alcohol driving simulator example to explore this. Imagine we test our participants in the simulator twice, once after a placebo drink and once after alcohol. This will give us a two conditions within-subject design. We compare the number of errors they made between the two sessions.

The formula for this tests the difference in performance between conditions in comparison to the standard deviation of this difference. To get the difference we simply subtract one score from another:

Table 12.10 Calculating difference

Participant	Alcohol errors	Placebo errors	d (difference)
1	8	3	5
2	5	2	3
3	6	5	1
4	7	2	5

Participant	Alcohol errors	Placebo errors	d (difference)
5	8	1	7
6	4	2	2
7	3	4	-1
8	2	3	-1
9	6	4	2
10	1	3	-2

We then use the following formula

$$t = \frac{\bar{d}}{(SD_d/\sqrt{N})}$$

This is the mean difference divided by the standard deviation of the difference (the latter being divided by the square root of N).

Imagine we have 10 people completing each condition, and find a significant difference between conditions with more errors following alcohol (mean=5.0) compared to placebo (mean =2.8). We would write this up as:

There were significantly more driving errors in the alcohol condition
compared to the placebo condition t(9)=2.31, p= .046.

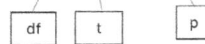

Again, the appropriate effect size would be Cohen's *d*.

Wilcoxon (Wilcoxon rank-sum test)

This is the non-parametric test for comparing two within-subjects groups. It doesn't make assumptions about the properties of the data, which means that is useful for ordinal data, smaller samples with non-normal distributions

Wilcoxon test. A non-parametric test used to compare two, within-subjects, conditions.

and/or big outliers. Again, it uses ranks of data although it does this by ranking the difference between the two conditions. Imagine that instead of measuring errors, we instead asked our participants how light-headed they felt consuming alcohol and after consuming the placebo drink using a 1(not at all)-5(very much so) Likert scale. This gives us ordinal data, therefore we must use a non-parametric test. We collect the data and it looks like this:

Table 12.11 Our ordinal data

Alcohol Lightheadedness	Placebo Lightheadedness
4	2
5	2
3	1
5	3
4	2
5	1
3	1
2	4
4	3
4	3

This test calculates a difference score (in the case alcohol condition – placebo condition) and then ranks the differences see Table 12.12.

For ease of explanation, I will put the differences into ascending order (ignoring if something is a minus figure), then rank them, then separate ranks out into positive and negative ranks see Table 12.13.

We then take the sums of the latter two columns (positive sum=50, negative sum =-5). The smallest of the ranks, in this case 5, is often used as the test statistic (W). However sometimes you will see a Z statistic reported I will report this in the example:

Lightheadedness scores were higher after alcohol compared to the control drink *(Z= 2.9, N=10, p=.025).*

Table 12.12 Our differences

Alcohol Lightheadedness	Placebo Lightheadedness	Difference
4	2	2
5	2	3
3	1	2
5	3	2
4	2	2
5	1	4
3	1	2
2	4	-2
4	3	1
4	3	1

Table 12.13 Our differences ranked and separated into positive and negative ranks

Difference (ordered)	Difference ranked	Positive rank differences	Negative rank differences
1	1.5	1.5	
1	1.5	1.5	
2	5	5	
2	5	5	
2	5	5	
2	5	5	
-2	-5		-5
3	8	8	
4	9.5	9.5	
4	9.5	9.5	

Often an r statistic is reported as the effect size for this test, which is the Z-statistic divided by the square root of the sample size.

More than two levels to the IV

Of course, you will often want to compare more than two conditions. For example, maybe in our driving simulation experiment, we add another condition:

* Alcohol
* Sleep deprived (no sleep in the last 24 hours)
* Control

How do we do this? You may think this is easy, we just do three t-tests:

* Alcohol vs. sleep-deprived
* Alcohol vs. control
* Sleep-deprived vs. control

But this produces a problem – the more testing that we do the more likely we are to get a false positive. We covered this in Chapter 9 in which we discussed how our critical value of p (p<.05) is changed if we do multiple testing:

3 tests: $1-(.95)^3 = .142926$

So in our example because of multiple testing, our critical p is essentially p<.143. This is a big problem.

All aboard the (omni)bus

We solve the problem with omnibus tests. These test if there is an overall effect of an IV (e.g. does our three-level IV affect driving errors in some way). It will give us a single p-value for it. If this omnibus test is significant, then you have a justification to test the differences between all the conditions separately (e.g. compare the three conditions as listed above). This is done with either *post hoc* tests or planned comparisons.

There are parametric versions of these omnibus tests (known as analysis of variance), and non-parametric versions too. We will briefly discuss themse all.

Analysis of variance (ANOVA)

Analysis of variance or as it is commonly called ANOVA, are parametric tests used to test the difference between three or more conditions. There is a

> **Analysis of variance (ANOVA).**
> Parametric tests used to test the difference between three or more conditions (within-subjects, between subjects or both).

between-subjects ANOVA and a within-subjects ANOVA and although the mathematics underpinning them is a bit different they essentially do the same thing and are reported in the same way. I'm just going to discuss the maths behind between-subjects ANOVA. You will be familiar with some of the concepts as it is just a form of regression.

We can think about ANOVA as the type of jigsaw my 18-month-old daughter does:

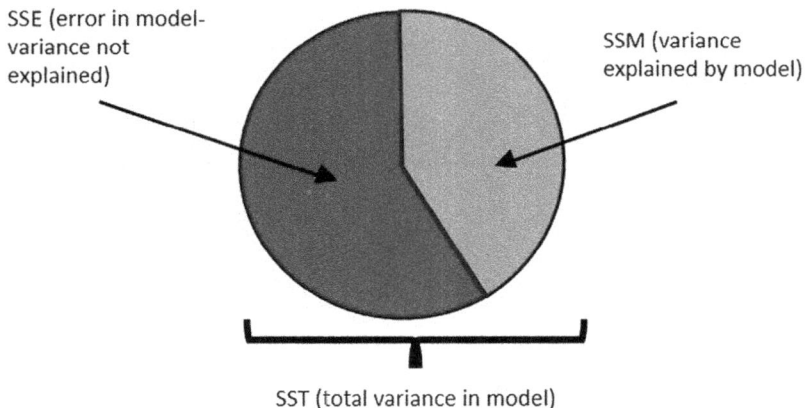

SSE (error in model- variance not explained)

SSM (variance explained by model)

SST (total variance in model)

Figure 12.2 My daughter's jigsaw/ ANOVA

The ANOVA simply partitions the variance in the dependent variable into variance the IV explains (Sum of squares – model; SSM) and variance it doesn't explain (some of square error; SSE). Remember most test statistics are simply looking at the proportion of variance that our IVs can explain. Finally, the sum of squares total (SST) is the total variance in the model is calculated as follows:

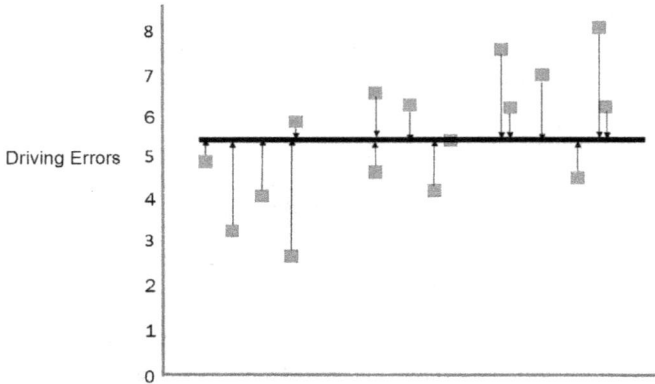

Figure 12.3 How the sum of squares total (SST) is calculated

We then look at the variation accounted for by the IVs, i.e. the model, this is SSM

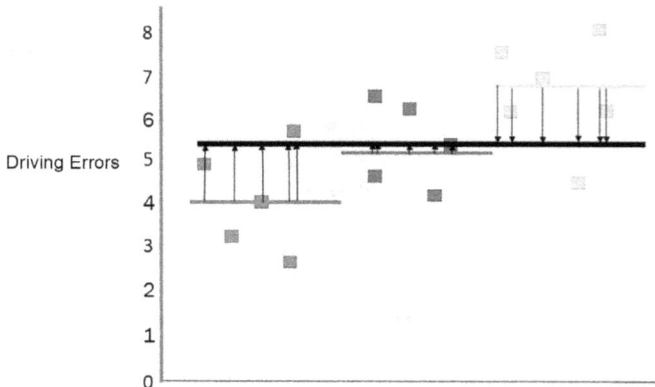

Figure 12.4 How the sum of squares model (SSM) is calculated

Mid grey (first short line) is the control condition, dark grey (second short line) is sleep deprived, and light grey (third short line) is alcohol. The formula for this calculation is:

$$SS_{Model=} \sum n_g(\bar{y}_i - \bar{y})^2$$

n_g = number of participants in that group.
$\bar{y}_I$ = mean of each group
$\bar{y}$ = grand mean (the black line)

This is simply how far apart the mean of each group is from the overall mean. The error for the model is calculated as:

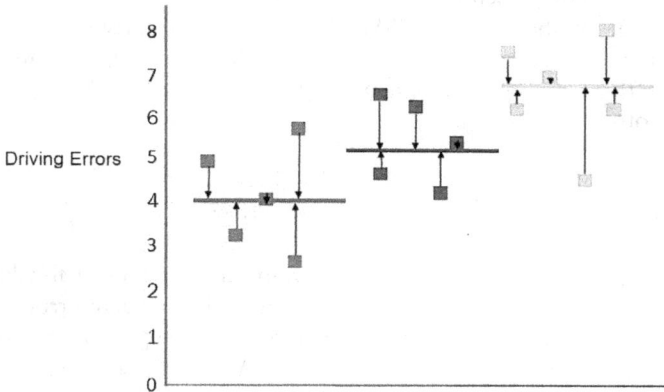

Figure 12.5 How the sum of squares error (SSE) is calculated

$$SS_{error} \sum (y_i - \bar{y}_i)^2$$

y_i = participant score in a group
$\bar{y}_i$ = group mean

This can be seen (in the case of a between-subjects design) as the within-group variation (how much variation in responses is there within each group) and is being caused by differences between participants in that group.

Using this information, we can calculate if there is a significant difference between the groups. We have:

• SSM = total variation that the model explains (between group variation)
• SSE = total variation due to unmeasured factors (within-group variation)

However, these two numbers had a different number of observations. SSM uses the difference between each group's mean and the overall mean, with three groups this is three observations. SSE compares the difference between each observation and the group mean. As there are multiple participants per group, the number of values used to calculate SSE is greater than when calculating SSM. This needs to be accounted for.

To do this the SSM and SSE are divided by their degrees of freedom (ANOVAs have two degrees of freedom):

- Degrees of freedom for SSM = k -1 (k = number of groups)
- Degrees of freedom for SSE = N – k (N = total sample size)

See how the SSE (which is made up of more observations) is divided by a much larger number than the SSM. This deals with this issue.

In our above example (with a tiny sample size – but it's just illustrative) we have three groups with five participants in each (i.e. N=15), so our degrees of freedom would be,

- Degrees of freedom for SSM = k-1 = 3–1 = 2
- Degrees of freedom for SSE = N – K = 15–3 = 12

By dividing the SSM and SSE by their respective degrees of freedom we produce the Mean square model (MSM) and Mean square error (MSE), this was done in the regression chapter too. Then we get to our last step, producing our test statistic, which, in ANOVA, is the F statistic.

$$F = \frac{MSM}{MSE}$$

A higher F statistic essentially means that your model (i.e. the IV) is explaining more variance in the DV than noise (individual differences). A higher F statistic means a smaller p-value. We report ANOVA by giving the F statistic, the two degrees of freedom, and the p-value. Let's say we had a bigger sample size than this example (it's really hard to draw the graphs I used with big samples!), with 30 participants in each group. My write-up would look something like this:

There was a significant effect of condition on errors, F(2,87)=16.77, p<.001

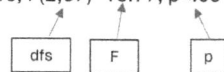

dfs   F   p

The effect size given with ANOVA is often eta squared (η^2), or partial eta squared η_p^2 if it has multiple IVs. These are often interpreted as, small $=.01$, medium $=.06$, large $=.14$. Notably, this statistic is broadly equivalent to R^2.

The ANOVA has told us, with a single p-value, if there is a significant difference between groups. Can you see the problem we have got here? We now know that there is a difference between the groups but we don't know *how* the groups differ specifically. We don't know if the most errors are in the control group compared to both sleep deprivation and alcohol conditions or maybe the alcohol condition has the most errors compared to the other two (or any combination of differences that you can think of!).

The ANOVA permits us to look at the differences between conditions, thus protecting us from false positives. If you do not have a significant ANOVA, you have no statistical justification for doing the following.

Post hoc testing

This is where we compare all the conditions:

> **Post hoc testing.** When following up significant effects in an ANOVA this is where we compare all the conditions.

- Alcohol vs. sleep-deprived
- Alcohol vs. control
- Sleep-deprived vs. control

There are some different methods of doing this, which I will not go into here, but they will produce a p-value for the differences. It is worth noting that sometimes people "correct" the p-value. For example, a Bonferroni correction. If you apply this in statistical software then your p-value will be multiplied by the number of comparisons made (i.e. it is "harder" for it to be significant). For example, imagine our p-value for alcohol vs. sleep deprived was .02; if a Bonferroni correction was applied to it the p-value would be multiplied by three, (as we are doing three comparisons, as listed above). The corrected p-value would become .06 so would now be non-significant. Of course, this method protects against false positives but elevates the chances of false negatives. For a good discussion on this see Chen, Feng and Yi, (2017).

Planned comparisons

Instead of every comparison you can test a few, scientifically driven comparisons. For example, I may only be

> **Planned comparisons.** When following up significant effects in an ANOVA this is where we make pre-specified comparisons.

interested in how sleep deprived and alcohol conditions differ from the control condition; leaving two comparisons. In this method conditions can be combined for comparison e.g. alcohol AND sleep deprived combined and compared to control. You need a good reason for choosing your comparison when doing these. You can also correct the p-values as discussed above.

Assumptions

ANOVA has some core assumptions, data should be interval or ratio (although it is often used on ordinal outcomes), and approximate normal distribution of data (this is not that important, particularly in large samples). Then we have a divergence depending on whether there is a within or between subject design.

Between subjects: Homogeneity of variance (relatively even variances within each condition) assessed with Levene's test. If this is violated two types of ANOVA deal with this, the Welch ANOVA and the Brown-Forsythe ANOVA (both are reported in the same way).

Within-subjects: Sphericity, this is a bit like homogeneity of variance but is whether the variances in the *differences* between conditions are consistent.

Sphericity. The assumption that the variances of the differences between all possible pairs of repeated measures conditions are relatively similar.

Table 12.14 Data meeting the assumption of sphericity

Participant	Control	Sleep deprived	Alcohol	Control- alcohol	Control-Sleep deprived	Sleep deprived- alcohol
1	10	10	11	-1	0	-1
2	12	11	13	-1	1	-2
3	5	3	3	2	2	0
4	3	5	4	-1	-2	1
5	10	12	11	-1	-2	1
			Variance	1.8	3.2	1.7

The variances in the differences (in bold) are relatively consistent, meaning we have met the assumption of sphericity.

Table 12.15 Data not meeting the assumption of sphericity

Participant	Control	Sleep deprived	Alcohol	Control- alcohol	Control-Sleep deprived	Sleep deprived- alcohol
1	7	6	11	-4	1	-5
2	10	3	13	-3	7	-10
3	12	10	5	-7	2	5
4	21	18	22	-1	3	-4
5	13	14	13	0	-1	1
			Variance	18.7	8.8	33.3

The variances in the differences (in bold) are relatively inconsistent, meaning we have not met the assumption of sphericity.

This is formally tested with Mauchley's test of sphericity (which you will want to be non-significant). Where you do not meet this assumption you can report corrected versions of the F statistic, most commonly the Greenhouse-Geisser correction (although there are others).

Non-parametric tests for three or more conditions

Kruskal-Wallis test

This is the non-parametric equivalent to the between-subjects ANOVA. I won't go into the maths on this one, suffice to say it involves ranking data. If you get a significant Kruskal Wallis test this permits you to do *post hoc* testing

> **Kruskal-Wallis test.** No parametric version of a between-subject ANOVA (with one IV).

(often using separate Mann-Whitney tests although Dunn's test is more appropriate). The test static for this is a Chi-Square statistic, and its degrees of freedom are simply K-1. Let's imagine our lightheaded ordinal example was used again and we found a significant difference. The test is written up as:

There was an effect of condition on self-reported Lightheadedness $X^2(2)$ =10.16, p=.006.

Freidman test

This is the non-parametric equivalent to the within-subjects ANOVA. Again, it simply involves ranking scores in conditions within each participant. As it's an

> **Friedman test.** No parametric version of a within-subject ANOVA (with one IV).

omnibus test a significant Friedman test permits you to do *post hoc* testing (often using separate Wilcoxon tests although a Conover test is more appropriate). Like the Kruskal Wallis test the test static is a Chi Square, and its degrees of freedom are simply K-1. It is written up as:

There was an effect of condition on self-reported Lightheadedness $X^2(2)$ =9.41, p=.009.

But what about multiple Independent variables?

When we have multiple independent variables we have what we call complex ANOVAs. We discussed these in Chapter 5, giving brief examples of such designs when both IVs are within-subjects, both IVs are between subjects and when one is between subjects and one is within-subjects (a mixed design). We also covered a specific example in a bit more detail in the chapter on quasi-experimental designs (Chapter 6). Let's recap this and then add how we would analyse this data:

In our Superphonics example, we could make a complex design with a between subjects factor of group (Superphonics vs. control) BUT also test the children *before and after* the intervention. This will let us know if our "Superphonics" intervention is improving reading while allowing us to be less concerned about pre-existing differences in class ability. The new independent variable would simply be "Time" (before intervention vs. after intervention). This means that we have a mixed design:

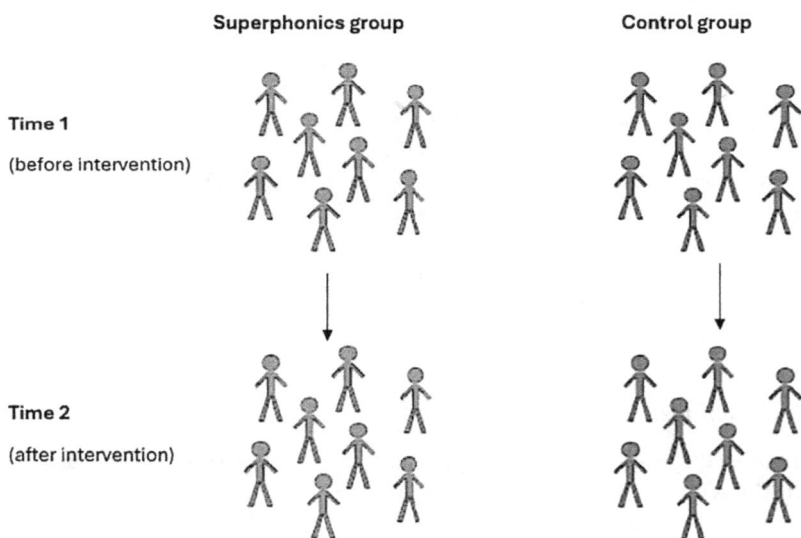

Figure 12.6 A pictorial representation of a mixed design

In this experiment, we have two IVs:

- Group (Superphonics, control)
- Time (before intervention, after intervention)

We run a complex ANOVA, and it will tell us the effect of each of these IVs separately. These are known as **main effects.** These are reported in the same way as they are for the univariate ANOVA. In this example, a significant main effect would not need *post hoc* testing. This is because there are only two conditions in our IVs, so if you find a significant main effect you know the two groups are significantly different (a *post hoc* test will tell you that the two groups are significantly different and give you the same p-value so is pointless!). If the IVs had more than two levels (e.g. if we did before intervention, after intervention plus a six-month follow-up), and the main effect was significant then we may wish to do *post hoc* testing of that effect.

The critical thing we would look for in this quasi-experiment is an **interaction** between time and reading condition. We would hypothesise that the improvement in performance over time would be greater in the Superphonics class compared to the control class. The ANOVA will test for this interaction and; again, this is reported in the same way as any other ANOVA we have discussed so far.

A significant interaction tells you that the two IVs work together in some way to influence the DV. Again, we can view a significant test statistic for an interaction as permission to do further testing, i.e. do *post hoc* tests. This means you have to explore the effects of one IV within the levels of another IV, e.g:

Those in the Superphonics condition:

• Compare before-intervention to after-intervention scores

Those in the control condition:

• Compare before-intervention to after-intervention scores

This will help explain what is producing the interaction. How you set up these *post hoc* tests depends on the wording of the research question. Like with main effects, there are different methods of post hoc testing of interactions, and there can be corrections applied to p values.

More independent variables

We can have more than two independent variables in an ANOVA. Imagine we have added a third IV, which we administer on a within subject basis-whether participants have had breakfast.

• Group (Superphonics, control)
• Time (before intervention, after intervention)
• Breakfast (had breakfast, did not have breakfast)

This gives us a 2x2x2 design, which means that we would assess with our test statistics:

- Three main effects

  a   Group
  b   Time
  c   Breakfast

- Three two-way interactions

  a   Group x time
  b   Group x breakfast
  c   Time x breakfast

- One three-way interaction

  a   Group x time x breakfast

The three-way interaction means that under one of the conditions the interaction between the remaining two conditions is different. I dislike three-way (or more) interactions as they are hard to do a power calculation for (work out how many participants you need) and can be *post hoc* tested in lots of different ways. When it comes to analysis, I think the **KISS** acronym should be remembered – **K**eep **I**t **S**imple **S**tupid!

Non-parametric complex ANOVAs

These simply do not exist! Friedman and Kruskal-Wallis tests only work with one IV.

Controlling for continuous variables

Sometimes you may want to control for interval/ratio variables that may influence your dependent variable. We can add these to an ANOVA, making it an ANCOVA (analysis of covariance), with the interval/ratio variable being the covariate. For example, in our

Analysis of covariance (ANCOVA). Parametric tests used to test the difference between three or more conditions (within-subject, between subjects or both) while controlling for a continuous variable.

alcohol and driving simulator studies we may want to control for how long our participants have been driving as this may be related to our DV (errors); those who have been driving for longer should make fewer errors. We report the covariates association with the DV using the same ANOVA statistics – although as it's continuous, we won't be able to do post hoc testing of it as there are no groups to compare. Doing this essentially controls for a "nuisance" effect on our DV, i.e. something we are not interested in. This improves the power of our analysis, as we have removed the nuisance variance associated with the covariate and now can look at a purer effect of the IV on the DV.

ANCOVA's have a key assumption – that the covariate does not differ systematically across the IV(s). If we have a between-subject variable of drink condition, and one of the groups has significantly more driving experience than the other, we cannot use driving experience as a covariate.

However, I guarantee you will come across a paper that uses an ANCOVA and justifies the covariates use as "because our groups significantly differed on variable X we included X as a covariate in our analysis" this is an immediate red flag in an analysis (and therefore good for critical evaluation). For a discussion of this, see Miller and Chapman (2001) and Eersel et al, (2017).

"MANOVA"-board (just let him drown): Multiple DVs and bad solutions

Finally, there may be a situation where we have multiple dependent variables and a set amount of IVs. For example, we may break down driving errors into,

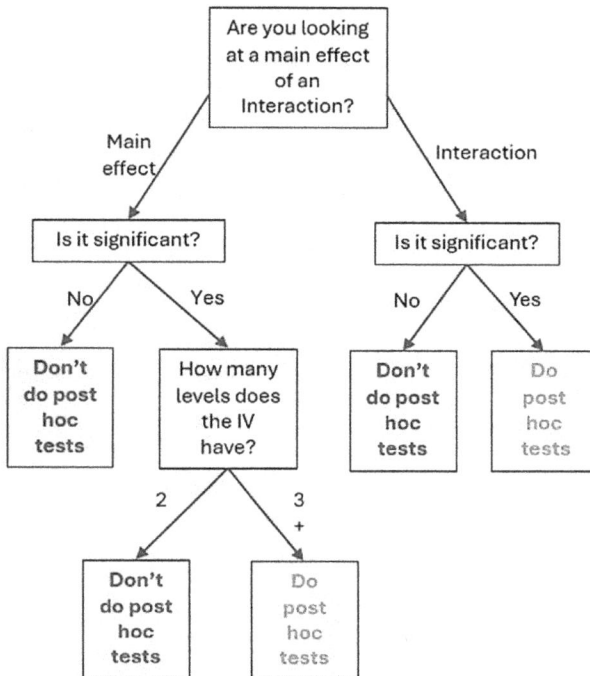

Figure 12.7 Should I do post hoc tests? A decision tree

failures to respond to road signs, steering errors, and failures to check mirrors. In this scenario, you could use a multivariate analysis of variance (MANOVA), as this gives you an omnibus test for the effect of the IV(s) on all the DVs considered together, if significant you have "permission" to look at separate ANOVAs for each DV. However, it has been argued that such tests are problematic and the likelihood of you satisfying all the necessary constraints to run these tests and get robust results is so small they are not worth considering. Instead, you should just run univariate ANOVAs on the DVs separately (if you are concerned about false positives you can do a correction on the p values for the ANOVAs). For more information on this see Huang, (2020) and Baguley, (2012).

Conclusion

It's over! There are lots of different ways to compare means and the method you use depends on your design of study and the type of data that you have. If you treat your data with respect (analyse it appropriately) then you will get results that you can respect! Remember what we are doing generally boils down to some sort of linear model. I'm sure you found ANOVAs the most challenging here, and don't worry, everyone does! You just need to have a bit of practice understanding them. Remember, if you see a complicated ANOVA with four IVs (e.g. a 4 x 4 x 2 x 2 design) and can't make a head or tail of what the author is talking about, don't worry as I'm 99% certain that they won't know what they are talking about either! If you are unsure whether you need to do post hoc tests on an ANOVA use my simple guide in Figure 12.7.

Further Reading

See my (Professor Paul Christiansen) Youtube channel for video guides in data analysis covering three different software (SPSS, R and JASP) https://www.youtube.com/channel/UCpjsdW-snzkUAx0lvqTJ7WA.

Field, A. (2024). *Discovering statistics using IBM SPSS statistics / R*. Sage publications limited.

Miller, G. A., & Chapman, J. P. (2001). Misunderstanding analysis of covariance. *Journal of abnormal psychology*, 110(1), 40.

References

Baguley, T. (2012). *Serious Stat: A guide to advanced statistics for the behavioral sciences*. Bloomsbury publishing.

Chen, S. Y., Feng, Z., & Yi, X. (2017). A general introduction to adjustment for multiple comparisons. *Journal of thoracic disease*, 9(6), 1725.

Huang, F. L. (2020). MANOVA: A procedure whose time has passed?. *Gifted Child Quarterly*, 64(1), 56–60.

Le Quéau, P., Labarthe F., & Zerbib, O. (2017). *Analyse de données quantitatives en sciences humaines et sociales* [*Mooc*]. France Université Numérique.

Miller, G. A., & Chapman, J. P. (2001). Misunderstanding analysis of covariance. *Journal of abnormal psychology*, 110(1), 40.

van Eersel, G., Bouwmeester, S., Verkoeijen, P., & Polak, M. (2017). *The misuse of ANCOVA in neuroimaging studies.*

Section 4

Key Impacts on Research or Practice and Policy: What wider impact has this topic had on the field/other fields/practice/policy

At the end of Section 4, you will

4.1 Gain knowledge of how using robust quantitative methods can make us more confident that our findings can apply to the real world.
4.2 Be familiar with the concept of reliability and why it is important.

DOI: 10.4324/9781032656564-16

Chapter 13

Robust quantitative methods and external validity of studies

Introduction

This chapter will describe how using robust quantitative methods can make us more confident that research can be applied to the real world. First, it will describe the concept of ecological validity, before showing (using familiar examples) how we can increase confidence that our findings apply to the real world. For example, how using probabilistic sampling methods can make us more confident that a study finding will generalise to the broader population. This chapter will compare some studies with good and bad ecological validity before discussing the triangulation of methods to ensure ecological validity.

External validity

External validity is a broad concept in quantitative research. It concerns how applicable results are to other contexts, populations, and times. If we have high external validity, that means that the findings of a study are likely to apply across a range of different contexts. If we have low external validity, this would mean that we would not be comfortable extrapolating our findings beyond the specific context of our experiment.

External validity can be broken down into different components:

- **Ecological Validity: The extent to which the study reflects the real world**
- **Population Validity: The extent to which the study's findings can be applied to a wider population than the sample used in the study**
- **Temporal Validity: The extent to which the study's findings can be applied across time**

DOI: 10.4324/9781032656564-17

We will discuss each of these in turn but the biggest focus will be on eco-logical validity as we have covered population validity (Chapters 8 and 10), while temporal validity can be a very difficult thing to deal with!

Ecological Validity

An ecologically valid study must reflect the real world. By this, I mean that the process being studied (both the IVs and the DVs) should reflect how these things are experienced in

> **Ecological validity.** The extent to which the study reflects the real world.

the real world. Of course, it is not just the direct manipulation of IVs or measurement of a DV that contributes to ecological validity; the broad context in which the study occurs is also important. Let's use our example experiments as a lens to explore ecological validity.

Alcohol and driving simulator experiment

In this experiment, participants consume alcohol or a placebo drink and then take part in a driving simulation where we count the number of errors that they make. If our study has ecological validity, this would mean that we would be confident that our study would reflect how people who drink and drive would perform in the real world. There are some things that we will need to consider:

The independent variable

Because we are administering a psychoactive substance we automatically get high ecological validity. This is because alcohol will have broadly the same influence on functioning in a laboratory and the real world. But we would need to make some considerations around the administration of this drink. The pattern of alcohol intoxication will differ depending on how fast a drink is consumed and how strong it is.

We could administer the same amount of alcohol in different ways:

- 37.5% ABV strength alcohol, in five 25ml "shots" consumed con-secutively in 5 minutes
- 37.5% ABV strength alcohol, 125ml of alcohol the alcohol mixed with cola (1:4 alcohol, cola ratio) consumed over an hour

Our participants will have consumed the same amount of alcohol (5 UK units) but they will show a different pattern of intoxication. In the first example, participants will feel intoxicated much faster than in the second example. So we need to consider this when setting up the study while asking ourselves which is the most ecologically valid version. We can argue that the second is more ecologically valid: few people consume alcohol by consuming shots in quick succession.

The dependent variable

This is really important in this experiment. We are interested in driving errors, so how can we measure driving?

1   Drive a real car around on roads with real motorists, errors are noted by a passenger (dual control car with an experienced driving instructor; Jongen et al., 2018).
2   Closed course driving, drive a real car around a course, errors are noted by a passenger (in a dual control car; Starmer 1989).
3   Driving simulator, participants sit on their own in a driving simulator and errors are automatically coded (Mets et al., 2011).
4   Computer tasks that measure things important in driving, e.g. reaction time, attention etc (Moskowitz, et al., 2000).

We can judge these in terms of ecological validity by understanding how well they represent real driving. Number one in the list is the best option as it is a real driving so represents the real world (almost) perfectly. The issue here is one of ethics; it is unethical to send intoxicated drivers out on the road. Number two, closed-course driving is realistic in terms of there being in a real car, but there are no other drivers there. So while you may make a realistic course, you would need to pay possibly hundreds of research assistants to drive cars around to make it realistic! Number three, a simulator, will depend on how good the simulator is. If it is essentially just like a car, with images projected onto all the windows and mirrors then it may be pretty realistic (immersive simulator). However, if it is in a lab with a gaming steering wheel and pedals and a single screen it would be less realistic, especially if there is no sensation of movement for the participant. The final example of using tasks involved with driving would have very low ecological validity as there is no driving being done. This is not to say that this is useless though: if alcohol impairs reaction time it is reasonable to argue that this has relevance to real-world driving!

There is a clear difference in our dependent variable in terms of how we measure driving ability in terms of ecological validity. Although not definitive I would rank these as follows:

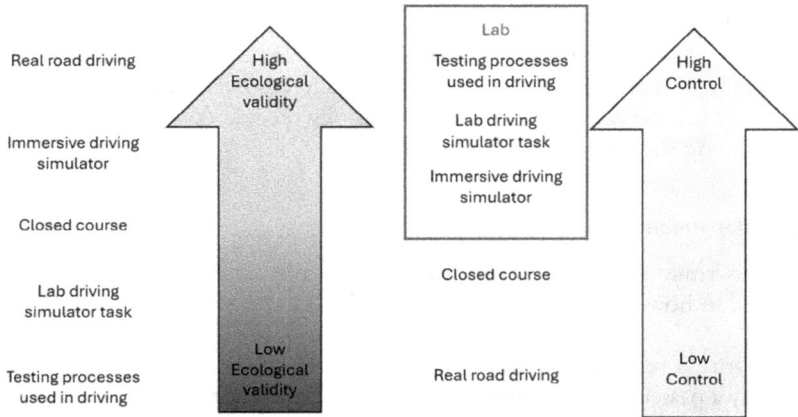

Figure 13.1 Ecological validity of the dependent variable vs. Control over the dependent variable

However, the drive for increased ecological validity in this instance gives us a problem. Our most ecologically valid measure is real road driving, and in this measure, we have to give up control of our testing environment. In experiments, we want control over other possible explanations for findings whereby the only thing that differs between groups should be IV. In real road driving, we have to give up a large degree of control; there will be different levels of traffic, people may hit a different number of red lights, and there might even be an absolute maniac swerving all around the road for one of our participants. Of course, we can control some things, for example, expected traffic density (fixed days and times to test), but even then, there is a degree of variance in these things that is out of our control. Whereas in the immersive simulator, we can ensure that our participants are exposed to the same driving conditions down to the which red lights they hit and the behaviour of other drivers.

If we compare ecological validity to the level of control, the order is almost opposite. Notably if the study is conducted in a lab we can have almost total control over extraneous variables.

"Superphonics" experiment

We are teaching children to read using phonics, but we have a new version of it called Superphonics, one group of children does this new version, and the other group of children does normal classes (control condition). Again, we will say it is a between-subject design.

The independent variable

The most ecologically valid way of doing it would be to simply deliver it in a normal classroom at the same time they would be doing their usual phonics class. In this way, the learning experience matches what they would normally do; the only difference is that they learn Superphonics as opposed to normal phonics.

However, this may not be possible: the intervention may be ten, hour-long sessions, and this could be deemed disruptive so the intervention (and the control condition) may have to be done intensely, so these ten sessions are crammed into two days. This would have lower ecological validity as it would be less reflective of the real-world learning experience for the children. If it was done over two days instead of in the usual manner students learn you could only state "Superphonics improves reading... *but only when delivered intensely*"

We may also want to consider who delivers the intervention. We have two options here: train the usual teachers to do it or get researchers to do it. The former is more ecologically valid as it reflects the natural teaching environment, but it has its problems. The researchers will be more familiar with the Superphonics intervention than the teachers so would likely be better at delivering it. So, like our previous example, this increased ecological validity may reduce control over the delivery of the IV.

The dependent variable

Our outcome will be reading ability. There are multiple ways to assess this with varying degrees of ecological validity. The most ecologically valid would be to look at reading ability improvements using standardised assessments that all schools use. Of course, this may be impractical, perhaps this assessment only occurs at the end of the school year and your experiment was done at the start of the year over five weeks, and by this time Superphonic effects could have disappeared.

Because of this, the dependent variable may have to be a test of reading performance that has been devised by the researchers. This would need to be carefully done, ensuring that it reflects best practice in the assessment of reading. Another thing that could be done would be a teacher-based rating of reading ability. This would be quick and easy but there could be biases, for example, confirmation effects whereby teachers may subconsciously rate those in the Superphonics condition as better.

Hopefully, it is clear what needs to be considered for ecological validity. It is important to remember that pushing for high ecological validity can sometimes cause other problems like a lack of control. When we lose control over our experiment and things other than our IV start to influence our results then we have issues in asserting causality.

Extrapolation problems: "IN MICE!"

It is really common for people to take findings and extrapolate them to far broader things. This is common in research papers, media or simply in conversation. This can be seen as an ecological validity issue. This is extremely common when people discuss pre-clinical work (which refers to animal models, usually mice).

There is a tendency for people to take animal work and extrapolate it to humans. For example, some studies show MDMA (ecstasy) produces neuronal damage like that seen in Parkinson's disease in mice (Costa et al., 2013). However, we can (very reasonably) argue that mice and humans are different so these findings may not translate to humans. But more critically, we can look at the dosages that are used in these studies, and if the animal dose is not reflective of human recreational use (with the animal doses being relatively higher and more frequent than human use) we cannot extrapolate findings to humans. Be careful when reading media articles that state "A new study has shown that substance X causes Y", ask yourself if you can extrapolate these findings to humans, and usually the answer is no!

Population Validity

This is whether the findings can be applied to a population other than the sample used in the study. I'm not going to go through this in much detail as we have covered this when we discussed sampling theory (Chapter 8) and methods (Chapter 10).

> **Population validity.** The extent to which the study's findings can be applied to a wider population than the sample used in the study.

If you have used a probability sampling technique then you will be able to apply your findings to the population that you have recruited from. However, if non-probability sampling has been used you are not able to do this to the same extent, your findings can only be said to apply to the sample you recruited. For example, it is really common for research to be done on undergraduate students, as these are a convenient sample for researchers who work at universities. We need to be careful about applying these findings to another population, undergraduate students are, on average, young adults of above-average intelligence and more likely to be middle-class. There can also be racial disparities between student samples and the general population. So for findings in such samples, you mustn't extrapolate them to broader populations too readily; again this could contribute to the critical evaluation of others' work.

Another issue that we could consider in applying results to new populations is something that is a pet peeve of mine. Arbitrarily creating groups and then analysing these groups. Imagine I want to do my alcohol and driving experiment and decide I also want to have an additional IV of heavy vs. light drinkers. To do this, I (stupidly) decided to measure how many units of alcohol participants drink in an average week and then do a median split (those below the median being light drinkers, and those above being heavy drinkers). There is a population validity problem here. If I run the experiment again, it is more than likely my median will be different so some people who would have been light drinkers in study one may be classed as heavy drinkers in two; this means the findings I get in my study only specifically apply to the group I did my median split in!

Temporal Validity

This is a tough one to deal with. It refers to applying findings across time. We cannot guess what the future holds (despite what economists claim). So, it is

> **Temporal validity.** The extent to which the study's findings can be applied across time.

hard to set up a study with temporal validity in mind. For our Superphonics study to have temporal validity it would have to show the same results in the year 2030 as it does in 2025. The big interrupter of temporal validity can be things like big societal changes. If we have a study that explored attitudes towards cigarettes in adolescents in the 1990s, we may find that these findings do not extrapolate to the current decade because of big changes in public perception of smoking due to advertising bans, public health campaigns etc. Furthermore, developing technologies may change the validity of studies; again with the smoking example the ubiquity of e-cigarettes and their use by adolescents and young adults will alter perceptions of cigarettes. Another good example of technological changes making past studies less useful is the use of smartphones and social media. Kennamer (1987) describes how newspapers and TV influence voting intention. The research described in this paper is going to have low temporal validity due to people getting more information from smartphones and in particular social media.

Validated measures

When it comes to validity, it is important that "validated" measures are used. This refers to measures that have been developed to make sure that they measure the thing they say they measure in a given sample. In the next chapter, we will discuss this in more detail. To be brief, you must use measures that are going to work in your sample, if not, you cannot trust the findings, and if you cannot trust your findings how can you extrapolate them to the real world?

Triangulation of methods

This chapter highlights some of the challenges we have around validity (particularly ecological validity), and how there is often a trade-off between control and realism. Ideally, research uses multiple methods to answer broad research questions. So when studying the effect of alcohol on driving, I may wish to go through this process:

• Start highly controlled in a lab exploring if alcohol influences cognitive processes related to driving.

   a   I have lots of control here and can be very specific about the effects of alcohol on cognition
   b   But I acknowledge driving involves doing lots of processes at the same time so I cannot be sure of the broader effect alcohol has on driving

• So then I do a driving simulation study.

   a   Here I find impaired performance, so believe alcohol affects driving
   b   But I acknowledge that being in a simulator is not as realistic as real driving, there are more stimuli in the latter, and a simulator is risk-free

• So then I do the real-world driving study

   a   Here I find impaired performance too
   b   I can still acknowledge a limitation- having a codriver with dual controls reduces risk.

However, through multiple methods, I can be confident in my findings and argue my research program has given me an excellent understanding of the effects of alcohol on driving in highly controlled and more ecologically valid environments.

Conclusions

If we want our findings to be ecologically valid, we must use robust quantitative methods that allow us to understand psychological processes in the real world. Of course, it is not always possible to make a perfectly realistic experiment/study, but you can consider ecological validity through every step of research design to maximise it. Furthermore, when reading others' work you can consider ecological validity as it may offer a point of critical evaluation. A final thing: if you do a median split, I will find out what university you are studying at and change all your quantitative methods marks to zero!

Further Reading

Irwin, J. R., & McClelland, G. H. (2003). Negative consequences of dichotomizing continuous predictor variables. *Journal of marketing research*, 40(3), 366–371.

Steckler, A., & McLeroy, K. R. (2008). The importance of external validity. *American journal of public health*, 98(1), 9–10.

References

Costa, G., Frau, L., Wardas, J., Pinna, A., Plumitallo, A., & Morelli, M. (2013). MPTP-induced dopamine neuron degeneration and glia activation is potentiated in MDMA-pretreated mice. *Movement disorders*, 28(14), 1957–1965. https://borninbradford.nhs.uk/research/.

Irwin, J. R., & McClelland, G. H. (2003). Negative consequences of dichotomizing continuous predictor variables. *Journal of marketing research*, 40(3), 366–371.

Jongen, S., van der Sluiszen, N. N. J. J. M., Brown, D., & Vuurman, E. F. P. M. (2018). Single- and dual-task performance during on-the-road driving at a low and moderate dose of alcohol: A comparison between young novice and more experienced drivers. *Human psychopharmacology*, 33(3), e2661. https://doi.org/10.1002/hup.2661.

Kennamer, J. D. (1987). How media use during campaign affects the intent to vote. *Journalism quarterly*, 64(2–3),291–300.

Mets, M. A., Kuipers, E., de Senerpont Domis, L. M., Leenders, M., Olivier, B., & Verster, J. C. (2011). Effects of alcohol on highway driving in the STISIM driving simulator. *Human psychopharmacology: clinical and experimental*, 26(6), 434–439.

Moskowitz H, Burns M, Fiorentino D, Smiley A, Zador P. (2000) *Driver Characteristics and Impairment at Various BACs*, Report HS 809–075. N

Starmer, G. A. (1989) Effects of low to moderate doses of ethanol on human driving-related performance. In *Human Metabolism of Alcohol: Vol. 1 Pharmacokinetics, Medicolegal Aspects, and General Interest*, Crow, K. E. and Batt, D. R., eds, pp. 101–130. CRC Press, Boca Raton.

Chapter 14

Robust quantitative methods and reliability of studies

Introduction

In this chapter, we will consider the data that we collect and how we can ascertain if we can "trust" this data. By trust I mean, are we measuring what we think we are measuring and are we measuring it consistently? We will do this through a discussion of some key forms of reliability, test-retest reliability, interrater reliability and internal reliability, describing how these can lead to confidence in measurement. We will also discuss the consequences of low internal reliability.

Reliability

A reliable car always works, and a reliable car friend will always be there for you, but what about reliable research? To put it simply, reliable measures will produce the same results in the same circumstances.

For example, if I give you a questionnaire measuring how extroverted you are, I will want to be sure that the questions are all consistently measuring extraversion. I would also want your score on this scale to be similar if you did it at two different times. Maybe instead of getting you to complete a questionnaire measure of extraversion I observed your behaviour in a social environment and rated your level of extraversion; I would want my rating to be the same as someone else observing you at the same time.

These examples cover the three key measures of reliability that we will be covering in this chapter. See Figure 14.1 for the names.

Test-retest reliability

Stable traits

If running a study in which we are trying to measure a stable

Test-retest reliability. The extent to which a measure/instrument produces the same score across time.

DOI: 10.4324/9781032656564-18

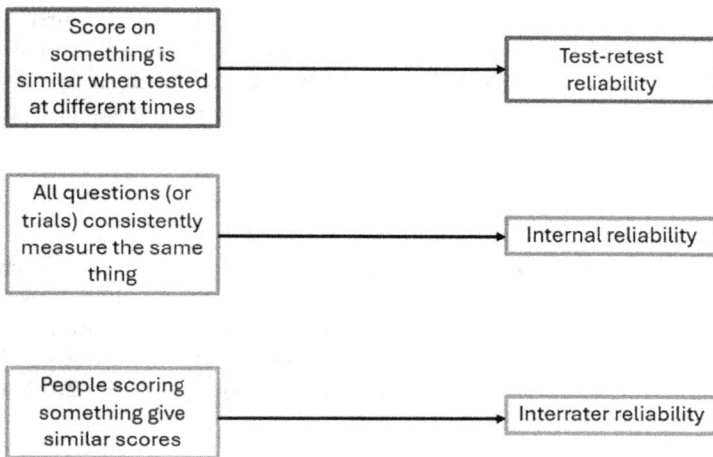

Figure 14.1 Measures of reliability

construct, such as a personality trait, a specific perceptual ability, or a form of intelligence, then we would want to use a task that is stable over time. If I have a measure of a personality trait that is not consistent over time, then it is probably not measuring a personality trait! If it is not measuring a personality trait then it is measuring something else, and this something else is not something that you are interested in! This is why test-retest reliability is important. It is a way of ensuring that we are measuring what we think we are.

Essentially if I believe that I am measuring something that should be relatively fixed (such as personality traits) then I would want consistent scores over time. Some things we believe to be relatively stable can change over time. For example, impulsivity (a personality trait) tends to decrease across the lifetime (Glicksohn, Naor-Ziv, and Leshem 2018). However, we can still assess this for test-retest reliability; we just need to assess it across a period in which we would not expect a detectable change, for example, two weeks.

Unstable states

It is important to note that for some things we do not expect consistency over time. For example, if I took a measure of current mood, this is a state (not a trait). Of course, some people are generally in better moods than others on average, but moods can fluctuate from minute to minute. That reminds me – **Pavlov walks into a bar. He hears a phone ring and says, "*Damn, I forgot to feed the dog.*"** You are probably in a much better mood now than you were when you first started reading this paragraph (because of my excellent psychology-related joke). Therefore, if I measured your mood before and after reading this paragraph then I probably would find inconsistent scores (or maybe I'm giving my joke too much credit). So, for things where we expect inconsistency (states) we would be less likely to be interested in test-retest reliability.

Measuring test-retest reliability

For some reason, when measuring test-retest reliability, lots of researchers' brains turn to mush and dribble out of their ears. This is not because it is hard to do! It is because people don't think properly (a running theme in reliability testing!). Indeed, people writing book chapters telling you how to do this often give bad advice (see Shou, Sellbom, and Chen (2022) who give the bad advice in the next section).

Pearson's r (don't you dare)

The problem with test-retest reliability is that people often assess this with a correlation coefficient, usually Pearson's r. Sounds sensible? From Chapter 11 you know that a correlation coefficient shows the association between two variables; so a strong correlation between two scores shows that when we test participants' scores across two time periods their scores are similar, right? Wrong! Let's imagine I take a measure of postpartum anxiety across two time points, my data looks like this:

Table 14.1 Scores from my test-retest reliability assessment of postpartum anxiety

Postpartum Anxiety: Time 1	Postpartum Anxiety: Time 2
1	11
5	15
3	13
2	12
4	14
2	12
5	15
6	16
8	18

Look at the raw scores, hopefully, you can see that the scores at time two are much higher than at time one. The Pearson's correlation between these two columns is one, there is a perfect positive correlation between the two! This would make you think that you have perfect test-retest reliability when you don't! This is a common mistake. For example, Weafer and colleagues (2013), conducted a study exploring test-retest reliability of different measures of impulsivity, and used a Pearson's correlation for them all. To date, this paper has been cited 299 times!

Intraclass correlation coefficient

There are a few options for assessing test-retest reliability. An intraclass correlation (ICC) is often reported. **This form of correlation allows the assessment of the difference between the scores.** There are different forms of ICC for different situations as it can be used for other things (such as interrater reliability), or for test-retest reliability when you have more than two measurements. For more details on this see the excellent paper by Koo and Li (2016). Generally, the guidelines for the cut-offs for an ICC are:

- <.5 = poor
- .5 to.75 = moderate
- .75 to.9 = good
- >.90 =excellent

> **Intraclass correlation coefficient (ICC).** A measure of test-retest reliability and interrater reliability (+other things!).

Repeatability coefficient (confusingly called CR)

This is an absolute reliability measure that considers random error as well as systematic error. It doesn't have cut-offs as it pro-

> **Repeatability coefficient.** A measure of test-retest reliability.

duces values based on the measurement (so will have different values depending on how a measure is scored). It provides the expected difference that you can expect between two measurements and 95% CIs for this difference. The lower the value the higher the repeatability. This is, at the moment, less commonly seen than the ICC.

Bland-Altman plot

The Bland-Altman plot shows the level of agreement between two measures, along with two standard deviations of the mean difference,

> **Bland-Altman plot.** A graphical assessment of test-retest reliability.

with the argument that you want 95% of data points (i.e. individual differences between values) to be within these two SDs.

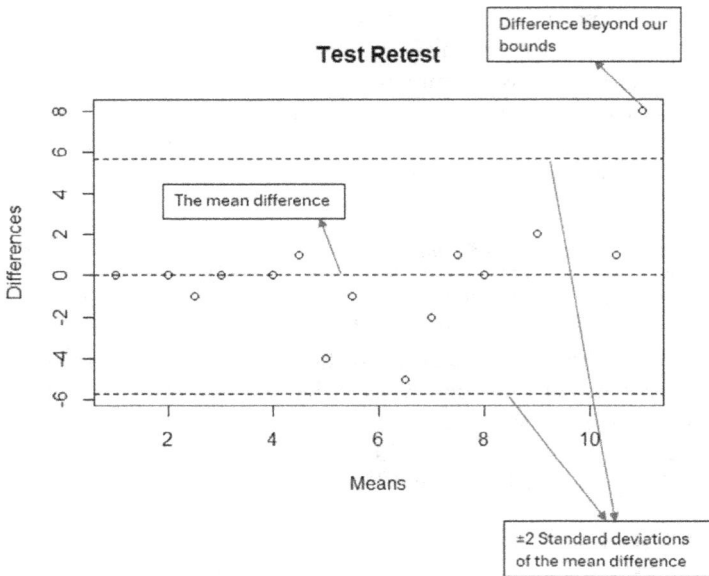

Figure 14.2 A Bland-Altman plot

In sum, test-retest reliability is really important but is often done badly. When you are choosing methods or evaluating other work, make sure that you consider this important aspect of reliability.

Interrater reliability (IRR)

This is related to test-retest reliability, but we are looking at the differences between different individuals rating behaviour. This could be in a natural environment

Interrater reliability. The extent to which two or more people assessing the same thing give comparable assessments.

or a more controlled environment; what matters is that the participants aren't doing the responses twice (or more; like test re-test reliability) instead, there is one participant (or animal) and different people are assessing them.

For example, we have videos of police interrogations of prisoners and we may want to score the police officers on how well they use certain principles of effective interrogation. Before we analyse the data to test if effective interrogation yields useful information, we want to be sure that how we score these interviews is effective. To this end, we get two people to assess the same interrogations and test if they agree with each other on the extent

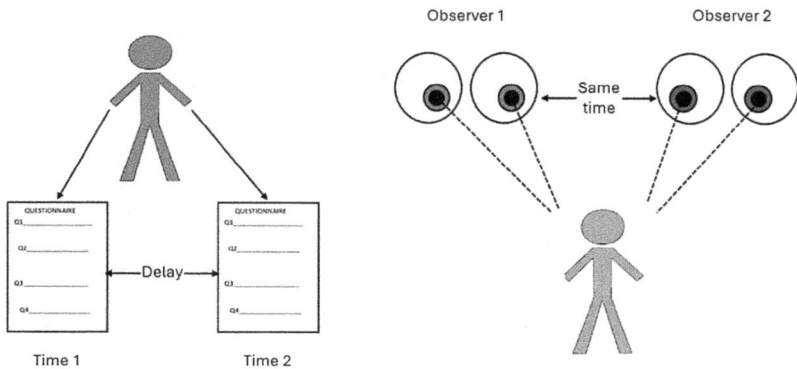

Figure 14.3 Test-retest vs. IRR (NOTE: terrifying floating eyeballs not necessary for IRR)

to which the police officers use the aforementioned principles of effective interrogation. Indeed, I have worked on a study that did this myself, see Surmon-Böhr et al. (2020; if you do read this paper, you will note I didn't get the memo about looking serious in the photo).

If we have two observers scoring behaviour very differently then we have a problem, it may be the measurement scale is not clear, or one of the raters is not very good at scoring (or they are both not very good). If you don't have interrater reliability how can you trust scores? If you have just one rater, how do you know you are scoring a true reflection of behaviour; your data could just be random guessing. Low interrater reliability would suggest findings are not replicable as variance in scores is not just due to the thing being measured but also who does the measuring! Assessment of interrater reliability depends on how things are being measured (i.e. the data levels).

Absolute agreement as a %.

This is used for nominal data and tells you the % of time scores are the same between two raters. This can be problematic when assessing rare events, for example, if I have two raters scoring people on having clinically significant postpartum anxiety and get the ratings in Table 14.2.

In this case, we have 80% agreement! That's pretty good, BUT the only two times clinically significant postpartum anxiety appears, it is for two different participants, i.e. when the event is stated to occur, there is no agreement. If something is rare it's easy to agree that it's not occurring! We cannot be confident in the ability of the raters to spot clinically significant postpartum anxiety here.

Table 14.2 Rare event interrater reliability for postpartum anxiety diagnoses in ten patients

Rater 1	*Rater 2*
Clinically significant postpartum anxiety	No postpartum anxiety
No postpartum anxiety	Clinically significant postpartum anxiety
No postpartum anxiety	No postpartum anxiety
No postpartum anxiety	No postpartum anxiety
No postpartum anxiety	No postpartum anxiety
No postpartum anxiety	No postpartum anxiety
No postpartum anxiety	No postpartum anxiety
No postpartum anxiety	No postpartum anxiety
No postpartum anxiety	No postpartum anxiety
No postpartum anxiety	No postpartum anxiety

Cohen's Kappa (κ) & Fleiss' Kappa

This is used with categorical data, it adjusts for the amount of agreement that could happen by chance. In contrast to the

Cohen's Kappa (κ) & Fleiss' Kappa. Measures of interrater reliability.

absolute agreement it often gives you poor scores when looking at low-frequency events. For example, the Cohen's Kappa for Table 14.2 is -.111. The cut-offs, according to Landis and Koch (1977) for Cohen's Kappa are:

- <0.20=poor
- 0.20–0.40= air
- 0.41–0.60=moderate
- 0.61–0.80=good
- 0.80+ near complete agreement

If you get 0 then the level of agreement is at chance levels, if less than 0 as in Table 14.2 this means that agreement is less than chance.

Table 14.3 None-rare event interrater reliability for postpartum anxiety diagnoses

Rater 1	*Rater 2*
Clinically significant postpartum anxiety	Clinically significant postpartum anxiety
No postpartum anxiety	Clinically significant postpartum anxiety
No postpartum anxiety	No postpartum anxiety
No postpartum anxiety	No postpartum anxiety
No postpartum anxiety	No postpartum anxiety
No postpartum anxiety	No postpartum anxiety

Rater 1	Rater 2
Clinically significant postpartum anxiety	Clinically significant postpartum anxiety
Clinically significant postpartum anxiety	Clinically significant postpartum anxiety
Clinically significant postpartum anxiety	Clinically significant postpartum anxiety
Clinically significant postpartum anxiety	Clinically significant postpartum anxiety

The example in Table 14.3 gives us a Kappa of 0.80 i.e. good agreement. It is notable that Cohen's Kappa only can be used if we have two raters, if we want to look across more raters then we have to use Fleiss' Kappa, which we interpret in the same way.

Intraclass Correlation Coefficient

When we want to look at interrater reliability for continuous measures we can use an ICC. This can be done for two raters or more (though a slightly different calculation underpins them). Again, the excellent Koo and Li (2016) paper gives more detail on this. We can interpret it just like we did for test-retest reliability.

Internal reliability

Internal reliability or internal consistency is the extent different items in a given test are assessing the same construct.

> **Internal reliability.** The extent to which items that are assumed to assess the same underlying construct or concept do so.

For example, let's look at the psychosocial adjustment to motherhood subscale of the postpartum-specific anxiety scale research short form (Davies et al., 2021). This subscale has four items that should tap into the construct of Psychosocial adjustment to motherhood. Participants respond on a four-point Lickert scale (strongly agree, agree, disagree, strongly disagree):

- I have felt that I have had less control over my day than before my baby was born
- I have felt unable to juggle motherhood with other responsibilities
- I have worried that I am not going to get enough sleep
- I have worried more about my finances than before my baby was born

If I want to take a score from this subscale (i.e. get a total score by adding up responses to these questions) I need to be confident that all the questions are tapping into the same thing. This is what internal reliability analysis does it ensures that all my items are measuring the same thing.

Although people often think about this in terms of questionnaires it is also an important concept in experimental tasks. Take an experiment using an emotional Stroop task. In a standard Stroop task (see Stroop, 1935), you give people a colour word (e.g. Red) that appears in another colour such as blue font, and participants have to suppress the automatic response to read the word to state the colour of the font. In an emotional Stroop, the words are emotion-related, for example, if we had an anxiety Stroop the words would be things like "Worry", "Fear" etc. Again, participants would need to react to the colour of the font. This would be done across numerous trials with an average time taken to name the colour of the font across the trials being the DV.

Let's think about the emotional Stroop in terms of internal reliability. Theoretically, this should tap into anxiety as more anxious people will have their attention grabbed, and held, by the anxiety-related words, as they are more salient to them. This means that reaction times to each word should be broadly similar as the task assumes that all the items (individual words) are tapping into the same construct, making an average score across all trials a valid measure. Problematically people rarely report reliability for such tasks, and when it is done there are often very mixed results (Brown et al., 2014; Field and Christiansen 2012; Ataya et al., 2012).

Measuring internal reliability

Cronbach's Alpha (α)

By far the most commonly reported measure of internal reliability. **Cronbach's alpha essentially tells you the average correlation between items** (although it is a bit

> **Cronbach's Alpha (α).** The most commonly reported measure of internal reliability.

more complicated than that mathematically). It has a maximum of 1 (everything having a perfect correlation with each other), and can be negative (this would mean that there are weak and some negative associations between items). If it is negative, then you are essentially asking for reliability stats for a set of unrelated items! For a detailed discussion, see Tavakol and Dennick, (2011).

It is often argued that .7+ represents the cut-off for acceptable reliability (Kline 1999) although some more detailed cut-offs have been used. For example, Nunnally and Bernstein (1994), suggest that.8 should be the cut-off for basic research and.95 for applied research while George and Mallery (2003) suggested the following cut-offs:

- <.5 = Unacceptable
- .5-.59 = Poor
- .6-.69 =Questionable
- .7-.79 =Acceptable
- .8-.89 = Good
- >.9 = Excellent

You will often see Cronbach's alpha reported in method sections of papers, sometimes it will be the figure taken from another study (e.g. when a scale or measure was initially validated) but it should be done for the current data in the paper. Indeed, if you do studies yourself using questionnaires, then you should calculate Cronbach's alpha yourself; it will demonstrate to those assessing your work you have considered reliability. If it is a good alpha then it is a strength for your study, if it is poor then it is a limitation to discuss.

Split-half reliability (Spearman-Brown correlation)

Also called the Spearman-Brown *Prophecy* formula (which makes it sound more impressive than it is). **In split-half reliability, a scale is simply split into two and the two halves are correlated with each other** (although there is a "correction" put on this so it's not like a standard Spearman correlation). Notably, there are different ways to split things. Even in our simple example, we could do the split in multiple different ways:

Split-half reliability. A measure of internal reliability.

For example, we could do the first half (bold) vs. the second half (italic)

- **I have felt that I have had less control over my day than before my baby was born**
- **I have felt unable to juggle motherhood with other responsibilities**
- *I have worried that I am not going to get enough sleep*
- *I have worried more about my finances than before my baby was born*

Or we could do odds (bold) vs. even (italic)

- **I have felt that I have had less control over my day than before my baby was born**
- *I have felt unable to juggle motherhood with other responsibilities*
- **I have worried that I am not going to get enough sleep**
- *I have worried more about my finances than before my baby was born*

Or we could take an average across the two. This is a very short subscale in our example. You may have a thirty-item scale. In this situation, there are a huge number of possible combinations for splitting your scale in two! Some software does them all and computes an average, others you choose how to split it. Generally, it is considered that a split-half reliability above .8 is acceptable.

McDonald's omega (ω_T)

McDonald's omega (total) is becoming are more common measure of internal reliability. **It is similar to Cronbach alpha and is usually interpreted with the same cut-offs but it does not assume something called Tau-equivalence (the association between each of the items and the thing they are believed to measure is the same).** It also doesn't assume error variances (the variance in the item responses not related to the thing being measured) are uncorrelated, nor is it a lower bound estimate. There is also a version of it called McDonald's omega hierarchical (ω_H) that deals with the problem I'm now going to describe below.

> **McDonald's omega (ωT).** A measure of internal reliability.

Pile up enough horse poo and it will smell like roses

Remember the definition of internal reliability? The extent different items in a given test are assessing the same construct. So essentially, are things we say are measuring the same thing associated with each other (which of course they should be)! Now sometimes people's brains stop working here too and they do something a bit silly. For example, this is taken from Schvey, Puhl and Brownell (2011):

> *Three-Factor Eating Questionnaire (TFEQ) ((24), (25)) is a 51-item self-report questionnaire that assesses restraint, disinhibition, and susceptibility to hunger. The reliability of the total measure in the present sample was $\alpha = 0.90$, and the reliability of the restraint, disinhibition, and hunger subscales were 0.77, 0.84, and 0.85, respectively.*

Pp1959

They describe three subscales, which measure different things (if they measured the same thing then there would be no need for subscales!), plus they compute an overall alpha across these subscales. Why? The items are not meant to be assessing the same construct! You will note, however, that Cronbach's alpha for the full scale is better than it is for the three separate subscales. This is because measures of internal reliability are biased upwards by more items. I would argue the reliability statistic given for the full scale is meaningless! Indeed doing such a thing can lead you to the untenable conclusion that although your subscales are not reliable (so don't each consistently measure the same thing), if you stick them all together they are reliable (and are consistently measuring the same thing!).

We can get a measure of reliability for a full scale though. The overall reliable variance in a multifactorial scale (known as "g") can be computed with McDonald's omega hierarchical (ω_H); this will tell you if there is an underlying factor (behind all the other factors) that is reliable.

The impact of reliability

The following formula is not often talked about but is important:

$$r_{(a,b)}(obs) = r_{(a,b)}(true)\sqrt{reliability_A \; reliability_B}$$

This tells us that the maximum observable (obs) correlation between two measures (A and B), is a function of the actual correlation between the two measures (true) and the reliability of the measures. This means that low reliability obscures the true correlation between measures.

Imagine that our postpartum anxiety measure has a Cronbach's alpha of .7 (so acceptable). My fear of childbirth measure is poor with a Cronbach's alpha of .5. I want to correlate these two measures, and the true correlation between them should be high, r=.9. We can enter the numbers into this formula. We will call postpartum anxiety A and fear of childbirth B.

$$r_{(a,b)}(obs) = .9\sqrt{.7x.5}$$

$$.53 = .9\sqrt{.7x.5}$$

Although the two measures should be correlated at r=.9, the reliabilities of these measures mean that the maximum observations we can see is r=.53. Quite a drop off! If you look at some of the reliabilities for some measures in Ataya et al. (2012), cited earlier, you will see some low reliabilities (e.g. 0.09). This has real implications for any study using such measures because you are unlikely to find any associations when using them!

Conclusions

Hopefully, you now have a good understanding of what we mean by reliability in quantitative research. Different forms of reliability are really important considerations when both designing an experiment and evaluating other work. We need to be confident that what we are measuring is (A) measuring what we think it is and (B) measuring it well. If it doesn't do both of these things, then how can we trust any hypothesis testing that uses these measures? I would argue that these are often not considered enough by psychologists, but if you understand reliability and why it matters, it will help you make better decisions around your research and understand the strengths and weaknesses of other research.

Further Reading

Koo, T. K., & Li, M. Y. (2016). A guideline of selecting and reporting intraclass correlation coefficients for reliability research. *Journal of chiropractic medicine*, 15(2), 155–163.

https://medium.com/@Sam_D_Parsons/ignoring-measurement-reliability-is-a-real-life-horror-story-b98a2517db26

References

Ataya, A. F., Adams, S., Mullings, E., Cooper, R. M., Attwood, A. S., & Munafò, M. R. (2012). Internal reliability of measures of substance-related cognitive bias. *Drug and alcohol dependence*, 121(1–2), 148–151.

Brown, H. M., Eley, T. C., Broeren, S., Macleod, C., Rinck, M. H. J. A., Hadwin, J. A., & Lester, K. J. (2014). Psychometric properties of reaction time based experimental paradigms measuring anxiety-related information-processing biases in children. *Journal of anxiety disorders*, 28(1), 97–107.

Davies, S. M., Christiansen, P., Harrold, J. A., Silverio, S. A., & Fallon, V. (2021). Creation and validation of the postpartum specific anxiety scale research short-form (PSAS-RSF). *Archives of women's mental health*, 24(6), 957–969.

Field, M., & Christiansen, P. (2012). Commentary on, 'Internal reliability of measures of substance-related cognitive bias'. *Drug and alcohol dependence*, 124(3), 189–190.

George, D., & Mallery, P. (2003). *SPSS for Windows step by step: A simple guide and reference*. 11.0 update (4th ed.). Boston: Allyn & Bacon.

Glicksohn, J., Naor-Ziv, R., & Leshem, R. (2018). Sensation seeking and risk-taking. In *Developmental pathways to disruptive, impulse-control and conduct disorders* (pp. 183–208). Academic Press.

Kline, P. (1999). *The handbook of psychological testing* (2nd ed.). London: Routledge.

Koo, T. K., & Li, M. Y. (2016). A guideline of selecting and reporting intraclass correlation coefficients for reliability research. *Journal of chiropractic medicine*, 15(2), 155–163.

Landis, J. R., & Koch, G. G. (1977). The measurement of observer agreement for categorical data. biometrics, 159–174.

Nunnally, J. C., & Bernstein, I. H. (1994). *Psychometric theory* (3rd ed.). New York: McGraw-Hill.

Schvey, N. A., Puhl, R. M., & Brownell, K. D. (2011). The impact of weight stigma on caloric consumption. *Obesity*, 19(10), 1957–1962.

Shou, Y., Sellbom, M., & Chen, H. F. (2022). Fundamentals of measurement in clinical psychology. In *Comprehensive clinical psychology* (pp. 13–35). Elsevier.

Stroop, J. R. (1935). Studies of interference in serial verbal reactions. *Journal of experimental psychology: General*, 18, 643–662.

Surmon-Böhr, F., Alison, L., Christiansen, P., & Alison, E. (2020). The right to silence and the permission to talk: Motivational interviewing and high-value detainees. *American Psychologist*, 75(7), 1011.

Tavakol, M., & Dennick, R. (2011). Making sense of Cronbach's alpha. *International journal of medical education*, 2, 53.

Weafer, J., Baggott, M. J., & de Wit, H. (2013). Test–retest reliability of behavioral measures of impulsive choice, impulsive action, and inattention. *Experimental and clinical psychopharmacology*, 21(6), 475.

Key Emerging Areas: Where is the research headed?

At the end of Section 5, you will

    5.1 Have a good understanding of the replication crisis in psychology.

    5.2 Know what methods are being developed to improve replicability.

    5.3 Become familiar with problems with inclusivity in research and its implications.

DOI: 10.4324/9781032656564-19

Chapter 15

Reproducibility crisis

Introduction

This chapter will discuss the replication crisis in psychology. First, we will discuss the publishing of research, problematic incentives, and challenges to publishing null findings. It will then debate a range of issues from poor scientific practice to fraud, and how these have made it difficult for findings to be replicated. Concepts like p-hacking and hypothesising after results are known (HARKing) will be described. We will show the evidence for these problems being at the heart of the reproducibility crisis. Finally, we will discuss how poorly conceived research and bad statistical practices such as failures to check assumptions, and other things considered in previous chapters can impact reproducibility.

Reproducibility

Reproducibility simply means the ability for a finding to be reproduced. You would think that if a study finds a significant effect, for example, there is a

> **Reproducibility.** The ability of a research finding to be reproduced.

significant effect of alcohol on driving simulator errors, then if someone was to run the study again they would find similar results. Of course, the original findings may have been spurious: remember null hypothesis significance testing can give false positives as it is based on probability. But what if findings simply cannot be reproduced even after many attempts? We then have a reproducibility crisis.

Several studies examined the extent to which findings can be replicated. For example, Camerer and colleagues (2018) evaluated the extent to which 21 social science studies published in the Journals "Nature" and "Science" (prestigious publications) could be replicated. They did this with larger sample sizes than the originals, finding that 62% of the studies had a

DOI: 10.4324/9781032656564-20

statistically significant effect that was consistent with the original, with effect sizes in these replications being about half as large as the originals. The Open Science Collaboration (2015) found an even lower percentage of successful replications in terms of statistically significant results, with a similar drop in effect sizes. This is not just confined to psychology other areas also have had problems with replication e.g. cancer research.

If science is being done properly, how can this happen? Well if it *is* being done properly then the explanation is likely due to journals selectively publishing results as well as publishing incentives.

The file draw effect

This simply refers to how difficult it is to publish null results (i.e. where no differences or associations are found). Null results are an incredibly important part of scientific progress; remember how we discussed conjectures and

> **File draw effect.** When null results are unpublished so other researchers do not know null studies in an area have been conducted.

refutations and revolutionary science in Chapter 3? We need to test theory to progress, if a theory isn't supported then we need to reconsider the theory. However, it is much more difficult to publish null results; journal editors or reviewers often view them as less interesting and likely to be cited by others, so they get rejected for publication. Therefore the literature is often biased towards studies that "work" at the expense of those that don't.

I had a personal experience of this during my PhD, I was using a task that was influenced by alcohol consumption in several studies (all from the same research group). However, I could never find an effect of alcohol on it. I met a fellow PhD student from that research group and told them about the issues I was having and was told *"Yes, it only works about 20% of the time, we only publish those that work"*. It's not surprising that it's hard to replicate findings when this happens! There is another aspect of publishing research that can contribute to reproducibility problems.

Publish or perish

Doing research is a career, of course, many people love doing research but it is still a job. To be successful it is important to publish your research. Indeed, things like promotion criteria and the chances of being successful in research grant applications are heavily dependent upon having published research. Often people talk about "publish or perish". If you don't get papers out there then you are going to lose your job!

This produces two, contradictory, incentives.

- *What's good for researchers?* Publishing lots of papers.
- *What's good for science?* Carefully produced research.

This results in a desire for researchers to publish as many papers as possible, and sometimes this is at the expense of quality. However, the pressure researchers have found themselves under may have produced some more insidious problems.

Hypothesising after results are known (HARKing)

How do we do science? We have a hypothesis, we collect data and then test this hypothesis. This is "deductive" reasoning, you test existing theories.

> **Hypothesising after results are known (HARKing).** Creating hypotheses after you have mined statistically significant effects in data.

But what if you collect data, then you see what the data shows then make a hypothesis that fits the data? This would be inductive reasoning, and largely this is not how we should be doing science (although there are situations where this can be done e.g. when doing initial exploratory research, for example, early stages in questionnaire development using a technique called exploratory factor analysis). **What you certainly shouldn't do is see where there are significant effects and then *pretend that you hypothesized this all along*! This is hypothesising after the results are known** (Kerr, 1998).

This gives a false impression that you did hypothesis-driven research. It increases the likelihood of false positives, indeed if you get a data set you can always mess with it enough to find a significant effect. This is summed up well by a quote attributed to Ronald Coase (1972 pp 14)

> " *If you torture the data long enough, it will confess.* "

This type of thing is very common but hard to detect. There have been notable cases where this thing appears to have happened. For example, a former professor at Cornell University had several papers retracted where there seems to be examples of this (see Lee, 2018 and Erasmus, Holman, and Ioannidis 2022). Indeed, this latter paper offers an excellent discussion of the broader issues covered in this chapter.

P-Hacking

A related concept is p-hacking; this is where we don't change the hypothesis but manipulate our data to support the hypothesis. The fact

> **P-Hacking.** Where data is manipulated to produce statistically significant results.

that it is hard to replicate findings is at least partial evidence of p hacking. Some studies have explored the frequency of different p values published across journals. Masicampo and colleagues (2012) looked at the distribution of 3000 p values reported in three psychology journals and found an increased prevalence at just under .05.

As you can see in Figure 15.1 there is a leap up away from the expected curve at just under .05, this could be due to bias in publishing or p-hacking. I do think it is worth noting that if sample size calculations are conducted with the critical level of p set to .05 then we may see this (although likely not as extreme) pattern of p values (although I suspect this result is not purely the product of that!).

Anyway, p-hacking is a real thing that plagues the psychology literature and it could be done in many different ways:

- Removing participants from the data for not particularly good reasons. For example, because they are outliers (extreme scores). This is common, but often hard to justify. If a value is feasible in the population why should it be removed? Also if analyses are run and outliers are removed and then run again until something significant is found that would be clear p-hacking.

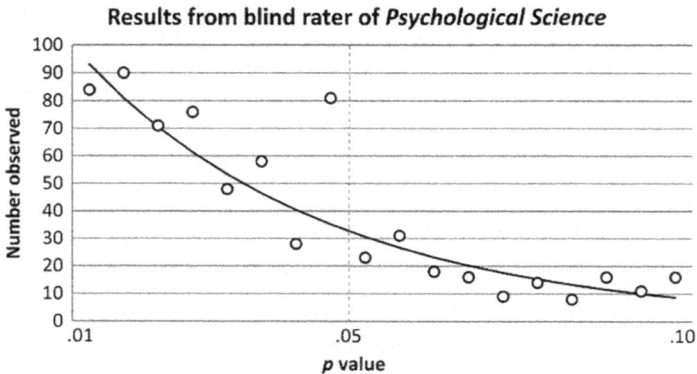

Figure 15.1 Distribution of p values from the journal Psychological Science taken from Masicampo et al., 2012.

- Needless transformations of data (sometimes people will transform data so that it meets certain assumptions). If this transformation is not legitimate or the researcher tries several different transformations until the results are significant then this would be an example of p-hacking.
- Controlling for different variables. I will use our driving simulator example for this. A researcher has an IV of drink (alcohol vs. placebo) and a DV of driving errors. They ran the analysis and found no evidence that alcohol influences the errors. They rerun the analysis:

  a   Controlling for Age
  b   Controlling for Sex
  c   Controlling for weekly units consumed
  d   Controlling for Age and Sex
  e   Controlling for Age and weekly units consumed
  f   etc

  Until they find a significant result. It is fine to control for things, but you should have planned to do this in advance, to keep playing with variables until you find something is p-hacking.
- Stopping data collection when statistical significance is reached. In this case, the researcher will collect data and then see if there is a significant effect, if not collect some more and check again until they find a significant effect. This essentially gives us the multiple testing problem, i.e. the more you test more likely you are to get a false positive, so doing this increases the likelihood that a "significant" finding is a false positive.
- Testing several variables and reporting the significant ones. For example, I may want to test if impulsivity predicts smoking in adolescents. I could take questionnaire measures of impulsivity, for example, the Barratt Impulsivity scales (Patton, Stanford, and Barratt 1995) which has three subscales, as well as the UPPS-P five-factor measure of impulsivity (Whiteside and Lynam, 2001). Then I could take behavioural measures (e.g. a Stop-Signal task, delay discounting task, Go-NoGo task, and an anti-saccade task). So, including questionnaire subscales, I have 12 measures of impulsivity. If I see which ones correlate with impulsivity and report only them then this would be p-hacking.
- Related to the above is changing the dependent variable. For example, if I ran a trial and had an objective measure of tiredness as the dependent variable and then changed the dependent variable to a subjective measure instead this would be p-hacking. Similar things like reducing the threshold to positive outcomes of a trial would be argued to be p hacking as well.
- Trends! It is common to see in the literature p values less than .1 ($p<.1$) referred to as trends, and then treated as though they are statistically

significant (e.g. a main effect in an ANOVA has a p-value of.08 so *post hoc* testing is done). This is another form of p-hacking and a big red flag. It is fun to see how people describe these p values (as they can't get away with calling them significant). I have seen:

a   On the cusp of significance
b   Nearly, but not quite, significant
c   Borderline significant

- Cherry-picking subgroups. In this case, researchers would decide, after finding no significant results, to reanalyse the data in different subgroups of people, for example only males, only those over the age of 40 etc.
- Sometimes, people will make arbitrary groups to analyse using median splits (those under the median go into one group those above the median another group), this should not be done, and there's a huge literature showing this (e.g. Maxwell and Delaney 1993; Altman 1994; Irwin and McClelland 2003), although it is still common. Indeed, if I conduct a very unscientific exploration of this and do a Google Scholar search for "median split" + "appetite" I get 143 results for the past nine months in this specific area of research. It is important to note that while it is a p-hacking technique this doesn't mean everyone using it is p-hacking! It could be done with a genuine belief that it is a good idea to do. This leads us to another reason for the reproducibility crisis, statistical errors.

Statistical errors

I think this is common. You may think that all researchers will understand quantitative methods, but believe me, this is far from the case! Many don't have training beyond what they did as undergraduates twenty or thirty years ago! Furthermore, statistics does not sit idle, there are newer techniques and a better understanding of statistical methods now. We often see outdated and incorrect statistical methods being used because people have always done it this way. Because papers are usually reviewed by people with a background in the subject area rather than statistics these problems get missed!

You will come across many statistical errors or problems in papers throughout your studies, don't be afraid to point them out. This may be analysing trends, median splits etc. This will be a nice critical evaluation.

Fraud

Now the truly unpleasant part of this- research fraud. There are now multiple examples of bad research practice that could be described as fraud. One example of this is (former) Professor Diederik Stapel who was a very successful academic, publishing research in some of the most prestigious journals and appearing on television. For example, "Coping with chaos: How disordered contexts promote stereotyping and discrimination" was published in the journal *Science*, and had a huge amount of press. The problem was the data was fabricated! This paper has since been retracted. After an investigation, he was found to have made up the data for several studies. There was a criminal prosecution resulting in community service. There are some other high-profile ongoing cases about accusations of research fraud currently rumbling on. It's really hard to spot fraud, although, with some things that we will discuss in the next chapter, it's harder to get away with it than it was in the past. The only lesson to be learned here is don't put people on pedestals, you may end up disappointed!

How big a problem is this?

It's big but getting smaller! In their seminal paper, John, Loewenstein and Prelec (2012) surveyed over 2000 psychologists in the US to assess the extent they admit to questionable research practices.

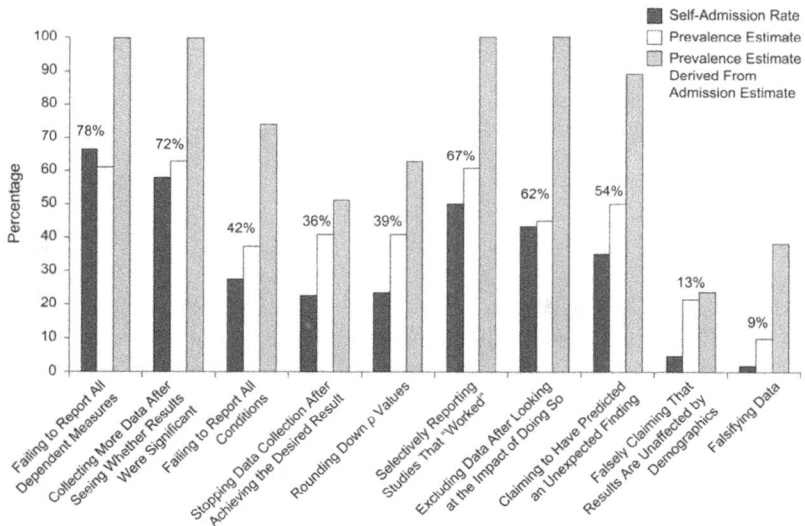

Figure 15.2 Self-admission rate, prevalence estimate, prevalence estimate derived from the admission estimate of questionable research practice. The % is the estimated mean across these three.

So, you can see the estimated prevalence of failing to report all dependent measures is 78%! While falsifying data is at 9%. This is a frightening situation! But it is critical to note that this was over ten years ago and this shocked the research community into some substantive change. In the next chapter, we will consider these changes and your role in this change!

Conclusion

Doom and despair! What have you got yourselves into? Well, first of all, most people are decent and honest, and often problems with research are just mistakes. However, there are problems in the literature and wider research. I would say to you that if you are asked to do something you feel crosses the line of ethical practice in research you should push back on it. It's also important to note that some great initiatives are improving reproducibility, which we will be discussing in the next chapter.

Further Reading

Masicampo E. J., & Lalande D. R. (2012). *A peculiar prevalence of p-values just below. 05. The quarterly journal of experimental psychology*, 65, 2271–2279.
John, L. K., Loewenstein, G., & Prelec, D. (2012). Measuring the prevalence of questionable research practices with incentives for truth telling. *Psychological science*, 23(5), 524–532.
A blog on the infamous PACE trial: https://www.rwkgoodman.com/info-hub/pa ce-trial-scandal-me-cfs/.
The Francesca Gino Case: https://www.newyorker.com/news/news-desk/how-a -scientific-dispute-spiralled-into-a-defamation-lawsuit.

References

Altman, D. G. (1994). Problems in dichotomizing continuous variables. *American journal of epidemiology*, 139(4), 442–442.
Camerer, C. F., Dreber, A., Holzmeister, F., Ho, T. H., Huber, J., Johannesson, M., ... & Wu, H. (2018). Evaluating the replicability of social science experiments in Nature and Science between 2010 and 2015. *Nature human behaviour*, 2(9), 637–644.
Erasmus, A., Holman, B., & Ioannidis, J. P. (2022). Data-dredging bias. *BMJ Evidence-Based Medicine*, 27(4), 209–211.
Good, I. J. (1972) Statistics and Today's Problems. *The American Statistician*, 26 (3). (Invited lecture at the 129th Meeting of the Institute of Mathematical Statistics on April 22, 1971), Start Page 11, Quote Page 14, Taylor & Francis, Abingdon, Oxfordshire, England. (JSTOR)

Irwin, J. R., and McClelland, G. H. (2003). Negative consequences of dichotomizing continuous predictor variables. *Journal of marketing research*, 40(3), 366–371.

John, L. K., Loewenstein, G., & Prelec, D. (2012). Measuring the prevalence of questionable research practices with incentives for truth telling. *Psychological science*, 23(5), 524–532.

Kerr, N. L. (1998). HARKing: Hypothesizing after the results are known. *Personality and social psychology review*, 2(3), 196–217.

Lee, S. (2018) https://centerforhealthjournalism.org/our-work/insights/emails-showed-how-famous-ivy-league-food-lab-was-cooking-shoddy-data.

Masicampo E. J., & Lalande D. R. (2012). *A peculiar prevalence of p-values just below. 05. The Quarterly Journal of Experimental Psychology*, 65, 2271–2279.

Maxwell, S. E., & Delaney, H. D. (1993). Bivariate median splits and spurious statistical significance. *Psychological bulletin*, 113(1), 181.

Open Science Collaboration. (2015). Estimating the reproducibility of psychological science. *Science*, 349(6251), aac4716.

Patton, J. H., Stanford, M. S., & Barratt, E. S. (1995). Factor structure of the Barratt impulsiveness scale. *Journal of clinical psychology*, 51(6), 768–774.

Stapel, D. A., & Lindenberg, S. (2011). Coping with chaos: How disordered contexts promote stereotyping and discrimination. *Science*, 332(6026), 251–253.

Whiteside, S. P., & Lynam, D. R. (2001). The five factor model and impulsivity: Using a structural model of personality to understand impulsivity. *Personality and individual differences*, 30(4), 669–689.

Chapter 16

Increasing reproducibility

Introduction

This chapter consists of guidance on how to increase reproducibility through open science initiatives. First, we will discuss the preregistration of studies, with a focus on aspredicted.org, showing how it can prevent the issues outlined in Chapter 15. Next, I will introduce you to the open science framework (OSF) with a particular emphasis on open data, before discussing how journals are trying to improve things with registered reports. Finally, there is an interview with Dr Charlotte Pennington the author of "A Students Guide to Open Science".

Preregistration

One of the best ways to improve reproducibility is preregistration of studies. **This means that you put down on a permanent record what your methods will be, as well as how you intend to analyse the data.** The presence of this record means that other researchers can check you have done what you originally planned. This is particularly good for stopping HARKing as intended hypotheses are clearly stated. It is also, at least partially, effective in preventing p-hacking as major deviations from the planned analysis would indicate that p-hacking may have occurred. Of course, no one will make people preregister studies and the majority of studies you read will not be preregistered, however, you can place more trust in preregistered work.

Preregistration. The act of putting on permanent record your research plans to ensure that no HARKing or P-hacking can take place.

Let's take a look at how we can preregister work using "as predicted" found at https://aspredicted.org/.

DOI: 10.4324/9781032656564-21

1) Data collection. Have any data been collected for this study? *This just asks you whether the data has already been collected.*

2) Hypothesis What's the main question being asked or hypothesis being tested in this study?

This prevents HARKing; you explicitly state what your hypothesis is going to be, and of course, you want your hypothesis to be specific and operationalised (just like we discussed in Chapter 3).

3) Dependent variable Describe the key dependent variable(s) specifying how they will be measured

This prevents having multiple possible DVs for example objective and subjective measures of fatigue and seeing which one significantly changes and just reporting that.

4) Conditions How many and which conditions will participants be assigned to?

This is where you can state the IVs (when comparing conditions). Again, this means that all conditions will have to be reported. Of course, in correlational research, you won't have conditions, but you could use this space to say what predictors you will have in your correlational study (although this could be done in the next section as well).

5) Analyses Specify exactly which analyses you will conduct to examine the main question/hypothesis.

Here you clearly state what you are doing to test your hypothesis, making the statistics you intend to use explicit. This prevents using multiple different analyses until you find the results you want, e.g. controlling for lots of variables until an effect is found.

6) Outliers and Exclusions Describe exactly how outliers will be defined and handled, and your precise rule(s) for excluding observations.

In this section, you state if there are any criteria for excluding points of data from analysis. For example, there may be scores on a test that would indicate that participants are suitable for exclusion, or perhaps if using an experimental task there may be certain aspects of performance such as reaction time that would be considered a reason to exclude (e.g. a reaction time over 2000ms on a trial may be excluded as you deem it to mean a loss of concentration). Some studies may have attention checks (for example a questionnaire has a question that says "respond with strongly agree to this question") anyone who fails this check could be excluded. This section ensures that people are not selectively pruning data until they find what they want.

7) Sample Size How many observations will be collected or what will determine sample size?

No need to justify the decision, but be precise about exactly how the number will be determined.

This is where you state how many participants you will recruit;, this could be through a formal sample size calculation or justified in another way. It may be as many as possible until a given cut-off date. This means that people can't keep checking data until they have a significant result.

8) Other Anything else you would like to pre-register?

(e.g., secondary analyses, variables collected for exploratory purposes, unusual analyses planned?)

Here you can add other things that you wish to explore. There may be a secondary analysis looking at a subgroup of your population you may wish to explore. This is fine to do but you need to state you are planning on doing this. A common critique of preregistration is that it stunts the "discovery" element of research, this section allows for this discovery element.

Hopefully, it is clear why preregistration is used. It can operate as a barrier to some of the activities we discussed in Chapter 15. As I said earlier, many people look much more positively at preregistered studies and sometimes they help stop null results from being a barrier to publication too. Take a look at aspredicted and see some preregistrations.

There is a problem though – it doesn't rule out dishonesty! People could say they abided by the preregistration but deleted certain participants anyway or fabricated data.

It's not my data, it's our data!

Another key initiative for improving reproducibility is open data. This means data is publicly available so other researchers can look at it and even use it in their studies. Interestingly, if data is made up then it is

> **Open data.** Data that is made accessible to anyone.

usually easily identified by statisticians, things look too perfect etc, so this immediately discourages that. This transparency means others can spot any errors in data processing or analysis that may lead to erroneous conclusions. It will also increase trust in research while at the same time motivating the owners of the data to ensure there are no errors at all; there's nothing like thinking someone will check your data and analysis to make you double-check.

Some universities have their own data repositories, as do some funders of research. However, the most common place to find data is on the Open Science Framework (OSF). This is a platform where people store all their research material including data, analysis code, materials and even drafts of work. Preregistration documents can be completed here, and it can be linked to aspredicted as well.

Registered reports

This is a journal-based initiative. Usually, you submit a complete paper (i.e. introduction, methods, results and discussion all completed) to a journal. Registered reports follow a different system.

> **Registered reports.** Publications that are accepted based on the introduction and methods (including analysis plan) regardless of what the results end up being.

Step 1: This is essentially a pre-registration although much more comprehensive. It will include a full introduction and methods section (including how data will be analysed). This is then subject to peer review. If it passes peer review it has an in-principle acceptance where the journal essentially says it will accept the paper regardless of the outcome. This also helps prevent the file draw effect (null results being harder to publish).

Step 2: This is the full submission. Data is analysed according to the plan and a discussion is written. It is peer-reviewed again but the acceptance is not contingent on the nature of the findings just that the analysis is in line with what is registered and the interpretation of the results is credible.

Like pre-registration, this is an excellent way to reduce poor research practice, although not that common at the moment it is gaining popularity. For an interesting discussion on this see Chambers and Tzavella (2022).

Be good at your job!

Statistical errors and poor analytical practices that stem from ignorance of quantitative methods are always going to cause problems. You can pre-register things, but if you preregister a load of rubbish, your findings are going to be a load of rubbish (although your heart was in the right place!). This is where taking the methodologies that underpin research seriously becomes so important. Anyone doing research should make sure they are up to date with quantitative methods and best practice as much as possible!

Talking with Dr Charlotte Pennington

Dr Charlotte Pennington is a Senior Lecturer in Psychology at Aston University and the author of "A Student's Guide to Open Science: Using the Replication Crisis to Reform Psychology" (2023). Here I get her experience of the replication crisis and open science initiatives.

PAUL CHRISTIANSEN: What was your inspiration to dedicate so much time to this?

CHARLOTTE PENNINGTON: It was because of my personal experiences of being a PhD student. In 2013, I embarked on a PhD that was investigating stereotype threat. This is a famous social psychological phenomenon which proposes that knowledge of negative societal stereotypes, such as women are bad at mathematics can influence their performance; there are over 300 studies in this area.

My PhD jumped in at the deep end to try and understand why was it that women were underperforming when they heard these negative stereotypes. Was it performance anxiety? Was it working memory deficits, or was it actually that they're motivated to try and disprove the stereotype?

I fell at the first hurdle because I could never get the typical stereotype threat effect. I had a hellish PhD experience because of this. I couldn't publish my studies because they were null. Peer reviewers were coming back saying that I must have missed something or there was a methodological flaw and in year two of my PhD I thought I needed to quit, I thought "This is me I am a bad scientist". Thankfully, my supervisor convinced me to stay and eventually, we did get some papers out, but it took a lot because we needed advanced statistics.

I joined Lancaster University in 2016 as a teaching associate, and I just wanted to focus my efforts on teaching for a few years and see whether I wanted to go back into research at all. There was an academic at Lancaster called Dermot Lynott (now at Maynooth University) and on his office door he had loads of stickers about questionable research practices and at the time it felt really scary. But Dermot invited me to an open research working group.

In one of the first workshops that they did, they outlined a brewing replication crisis and the influence of questionable research practices on research outcomes. And I just felt like a light had been shone into my world, which gave me the answers that I was looking for and made me realise that it was not me. That the field was quite a mess and everyone was talking about this in the corridors, but it was nothing you would ever see in the published literature.

We just see the tip of the iceberg. When you look at the published literature, it all looks rosy, but you don't see what's underneath the surface. And I think it's important to remember that this is normal because research is difficult and it's messy. But we need to be able to show people how messy it is as well.

PAUL CHRISTIANSEN: What do you think made us realise there is a replication problem?

CHARLOTTE PENNINGTON: I'd argue that some pivotal events happened around the same time, and because they happened around the same time, it caused public outcry.

Around 2011, there was a paper by Daryl Bem, published in a prestigious journal that provided evidence of precognition – a phenomenon whereby people can predict future events which are outside of the realms of what we know is humanly possible. But across nine experiments, Bem showed that people could predict a future memory task with above-chance accuracy. There was a team of researchers, Wagenmakers and colleagues, who just argued that it was too good to be true. What people don't tend to realise is that even when you're studying a real phenomenon, you will run into non-significant results. So if this was true, where were those non-significant results?

Around the same time you've then got Diedrich Staples who was the first person in psychology to admit data fabrication in his research. He's written an autobiography and it's eye-opening. It's a story about how pressures around research, egos, as well as wanting to be a superstar, led him down this dark path into research fraud. So I think those two things shed light on replication issues. It's important to note the Bem paper has never been found to be fraudulent, but I think that those two things happening at the same time really got people talking.

PAUL CHRISTIANSEN: Would you say things have got better over the last 10 years?

CHARLOTTE PENNINGTON: I would say absolutely yes, and because it's got better, this is why I am still in the field. I think the advent of open science has completely turned things around. Open science is an umbrella term which argues that knowledge of all kinds, where appropriate, should be transparent, open, replicable, reproducible, and cumulative, but also equal and represent the humans that we are studying, both in terms of our participants, but also the researchers who are in our field. And within that umbrella, there are many different practices that you have outlined in the chapter, such as study pre-registration.

I'm a real fan of study pre-registration - a protocol of what you're going to do before you go and do it. So when I was a PhD student I used to go out and collect data and then have a meeting with my supervisory team to try to work out how we were going to analyse the data. And now I look back at that and just think, I can't believe that that was even the world that we lived in because at that point you are biassed towards what you want to find. Pre-registration helps because it allows you to plan better studies, but it mitigates a lot of questionable research practices.

With registered reports, it's exactly the same as a study pre-registration, but experts in the field are vetting your protocol before you go out and collect your data. So registered reports split the peer review process in half. Regardless of the results, given that you stick to your protocol, you simply append the results and the discussion section to your stage 1 report. Publication bias can't play anymore because the journal said we don't care about results anymore. We care about methodological rigour, and I think that should have always been the case.

PAUL CHRISTIANSEN: When it comes to undergraduate students reading this – what can they do about it?

CHARLOTTE PENNINGTON: I think what is great about the replication crisis and open science is that it does improve student's critical thinking because they don't read a paper with all of their trust. They can look for the advantages and the disadvantages of that research paper. I think that if you are trained to know what open science practices are then you would be able to spot them. For example, a study may state that it was pre-registered and it will provide a link to the protocol, a student could click on that link in the paper and see this has been pre-registered.

I think the absence of open science practices makes you a little bit more critical now. The important thing to note here is that just because people don't engage in open science practises does not mean that that paper is inherently bad. Some researchers might still be using very responsible research practises, but they may not learned open science or felt confident enough to engage with it. So I would just be careful of kind of a blank conclusion that no open science equals bad science. I think it's important also to know that just because a study is pre-registered for example, doesn't mean that it's got the most perfect design and analysis plan you can still pre-register a completely shoddy research study.

PAUL CHRISTIANSEN: We have talked about problems, and I suppose a student could read this and say, "What's the point I can't trust anything", what would you say to a student who thinks is this just futile?

CHARLOTTE PENNINGTON: I was this person, I was very pessimistic about the state of our field. A lot of seminal studies that I'd grown up with and grew to love, such as stereotype threat, growth mindset, ego depletion, priming etc, seemed to have gone up in smoke. I think the first thing to note is it's really important to question everything.

I honestly think that open science has reformed our discipline and I've been questioning recently whether we still find ourselves in a replication crisis, or are we coming out the other end knowing that we've improved things? I think it's fascinating to understand that these issues are present across all of science. So replication and reproducibility issues are also present in the natural sciences, which people don't tend to pick up on, it's not just psychology. So it's not like you've made the wrong choice of what to study. What's amazing is that psychology has been a trailblazer for these new initiatives. And I suppose we've gone beyond the practices of pre-registration and open data to reflect on who is represented in science and who are we inviting to the table; thinking about diversity and equality initiatives. I think now it's a really lovely place to be and that students can get involved with open science as well. A lot of early career researchers have been the people to develop these initiatives.

PAUL CHRISTIANSEN: When students are doing their research, what should be at the top of their minds when it comes to reproducibility?

CHARLOTTE PENNINGTON: I think reflecting on your values and ethos as a researcher is really important. So do you want to implement open science practises and why do you want to do that? I think sitting down and knowing who you are is good and having some reflexivity in the research process is a very good thing to do. I would say also reflecting on the skills that you're learning in research and how they apply to the graduate world is important as well. Think about how an employer would value those skills. You might have set up a project, and developed your data management skills through open data (making data sets understandable and accessible); an employer would be excited to hear about that.

I suppose also thinking about your knowledge of ethics and social responsibility. So being a responsible researcher in that context is great for the world as well because it means that you're socially responsible. You think before you do, you evaluate well. And again, an employer would be keen to hear about this.

PAUL CHRISTIANSEN: That's a really good point it goes beyond research. This is about you, it's not only beneficial for research, it's beneficial for you as a person, and your career. Ultimately it makes you a better, more rounded person and surely that is one of the ultimate goals of university. it's not just a knowledge base, it is about growth. And I think that's an excellent point to end on.

Conclusion

Thanks to the efforts of many researchers, particularly early career researchers, we are in a much better position than we were ten years ago.

The initiatives we have discussed in this chapter are helping improve psychology as a science, and are all things you should look for in your reading. As you will see from my conversation with Dr Charlotte Pennington, you can get involved in doing things the right way from the outset of your career; indeed, you can be one of the change-makers in the field!

Further Reading

Pennington, C. (2023). *A student's guide to open science: Using the replication crisis to reform psychology.* McGraw-Hill Education (UK).

The full interview with Dr Pennington https://www.youtube.com/watch?v=X72iE8Rwwpo&t.

References

Bem, D. J. (2011). Feeling the future: experimental evidence for anomalous retroactive influences on cognition and affect. *Journal of personality and social psychology*, 100 (3), 407

Chambers, C. D., & Tzavella, L. (2022). The past, present and future of Registered Reports. *Nature human behaviour*, 6(1), 29–42.

Pennington, C. (2023). *A student's guide to open science: Using the replication crisis to reform psychology.* McGraw-Hill Education (UK).

Wagenmakers, E. J., Wetzels, R., Borsboom, D., & Van Der Maas, H. L. (2011). *Why psychologists must change the way they analyze their data: the case of psi: comment on Bem* (2011).

Chapter 17

Inclusivity in Research

Introduction

This final chapter will discuss inclusivity in research. Firstly, we will discuss how much research has used young, white, middle-class populations, and how this has arisen. Following this, there will be a discussion about under-served groups, i.e. those who appear less in research than population estimates would suggest, and the implications for research and its societal impact. Indeed, it is notable that many under-served groups often have things like high healthcare burdens, so they can be particularly important to health and clinical psychology. It will then pose a series of questions that a researcher may want to ask themselves if they wish to ensure that their research is inclusive. Finally, we will briefly cover how to talk to specific groups using person-first or identity-first language.

A WEIRD population

If you read enough research papers something really weird starts to become apparent – samples in these studies tend to be over-whelmingly white and middle-class. This is because the most con-

> **WEIRD samples.** Western, Educated, Industrialized, Rich, and Democratic samples that make up a considerable proportion of psychological research.

venient sample for European and US researchers to recruit from is their students. The university population in all these countries is biased towards being white and middle class. Indeed, if you take this a step further and look at psychology cohorts these are biased towards being white, middle class, and female. This is of course a problem, as we covered in Chapter 8; we want our sample to be representative of our population of interest.

How bad is this problem? A review of six psychology journals found that 96% of participants were from Western, industrialised countries (with these

DOI: 10.4324/9781032656564-22

countries only being around 14% of the world's population; Arnett, 2008). This means that serious questions must be asked about how well we can apply research beyond this incredibly narrow population.

Henrich, Heine, and Norenzayan (2010) described how much research in behavioural sciences (including psychology) is based on **Western, Educated, Industrialized, Rich, and Democratic (WEIRD) samples**. They argue that this means that findings are unrepresentative. Indeed they give compelling evidence that across a range of areas, there are no universal psychological "truths" that can be applied across different populations. Of course, this is probably expected to be the case in several areas, for example in our fear of childbirth and postpartum anxiety study, we would expect there to be cultural differences in both these things. But you may think that for certain things like visual illusions that our perceptual systems are so similar we need not think about this problem – but you will be wrong!

Henrich and colleagues describe the work of Segall et al. (1966) that explored cross-cultural differences in the Muller-Lyer illusion (Figure 17.1).

Segall and colleagues found the Point of Subjective Equality (PSE); how much longer line B must be before it is perceived as the same length as line A differed across different groups, to a considerable extent. This suggests that we need to take cultural differences seriously across all aspects of psychological research.

Personality type –WEIRD

Another good example of the problems that are caused by WEIRD samples is that of the formal measurement of personality. You have probably heard of "The Big Five" personality traits (openness, conscientiousness, extraversion, agreeableness, and neuroticism). This is one of the most used personality taxonomies in psychological research, with many variations of the scales. The Big Five Inventory (BFI) is a questionnaire that aims to measure these traits. However, often when this is applied to different societies it

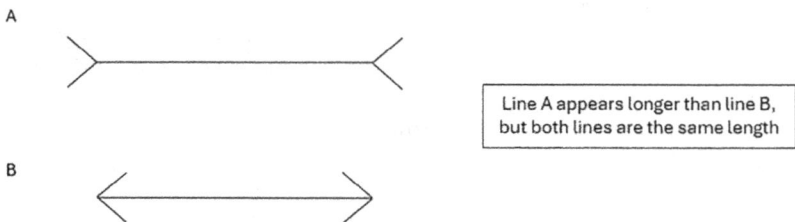

Figure 17.1 The Muller-Lyer illusion

fails to perform well as a scale For example in the "Ache", a group of people indigenous to eastern Paraguay, the reliability of the big five inventory is poor and its factor structure (i.e. what the questions were thought to measure) did not map on to the big five structure (Bailey et al., 2013), with similar problems reported with forager-farmers in Bolivia (Gurven et al., 2013).

Indeed, this is a big problem regarding scales. Many measures are developed in one population but are applied to other populations without formal validation (or at best incomplete validation).

Underserved groups

When we do research we want our sample to be as representative of the population of interest as possible. For example, I want to study attitudes towards COVID-19 vaccination in Liverpool (just because I write this sitting in Liverpool – any city would do!). I want equal representation of ethnic groups. Therefore I get the most recent census data and try and ensure my sample matches this.

> **Underserved groups.** Hard to recruit groups in our population who often will not appear in research.

This is where we can run into problems, some groups may be harder to recruit than others, these are called underserved groups. There may be many reasons for this, for example, language barriers, lack of trust in authorities, and the digital divide (if my survey is online then we may miss out on those without internet access).

Being unable to recruit from these groups has important implications. Several long-term health conditions are more prevalent in minority ethnic groups (Hayanga, Stafford, and Becares, 2023). So if we are doing health research then we have a bit of a problem in that we are not getting data from what may be a particularly important group. In our specific example, there is evidence that there are racial differences in vaccine hesitancy (e.g. Robertson et al., 2021) as well as COVID outcomes (e.g. Mackey et al., 2021; Raleigh, 2022).

There are many examples of underserved groups:

- People with mental health difficulties
- Pregnant people
- Carers
- People living in remote areas
- People with low income
- People with physical disabilities

Many of these represent sizeable portions of our population!

We can stretch the concept of underserved groups further to hard-to-reach groups. What if we were interested in people who are homeless, or have severe drug dependence? These groups are incredibly hard to reach. Take the former, how are they going to complete a survey, how would you contact them? Random sampling is nearly impossible in such groups, but some techniques could be used to target these groups.

Recruiting underserved groups

The National Institute for Health Care Research (NIHR) produced the INCLUDE project that developed advice on underserved groups. This is a useful resource for researchers in health research and beyond. They flag six questions you should ask if you wish to do inclusive research:

1   What are the characteristics/demographics of the population which your research looks to serve?
    Understand the population so you can ensure representation of the population.
2   How will your inclusion/exclusion criteria enable your trial population to match the population that you aim to serve?
    When selecting these criteria how are they going to impact representation; for example, you may have "unable to understand English" as an exclusion criterion, and the impact of this on underserved groups should be addressed.
3   Justify any difference between your projected trial population and the population you aim to serve
    If you are not going to be able to get a representative sample, then you need to justify it. Of course, particularly at undergraduate level, there may be very pragmatic reasons for this (e.g. you cannot get information translated other than at great expense).
4   How will your recruitment and retention methods engage with under-served groups?
    If you are going to ensure that under-served groups are recruited what is your strategy going to be, perhaps there is online guidance already, or maybe you need to speak to someone from these groups to get an under-standing of the best approach to take.
5   What evidence have you that your intervention is feasible and accessible to a broad range of patients in the populations that your research seeks to serve?
    This may be less relevant to us as this focuses on health interventions, but it is an important point; any intervention, to apply to a broad population, should work across the groups within this population.

6   Are your outcomes validated and relevant to a broad range of patients in the populations that your research seeks to serve?
This relates to one of the earlier points in the chapter, have the measures been validated in the different groups you are recruiting, if not and you still intend to use them, you may want to validate them yourself as part of your research.

Asking yourself these questions (and asking these questions of the research you are reading!) can help you improve your study design ensuring it is inclusive (or critically evaluate other research in terms of inclusivity).

Person-first or identity-first language

We should be mindful of how we communicate with different groups of people. There is a lot of stigmatisation associated with different groups and to ensure inclusivity we need to make sure that we sensitively communicate with them. We can think about how we address specific groups in two different ways:

Person first language

In this, we identify the person before the group they belong to. For example, in research into weight management, we would say people with/living with obesity, not obese people. The argument behind this way of writing is that people should not be defined by this characteristic e.g. their primary identifier is not being obese, it is being a person, who happens to be obese. Indeed, in appetite and obesity research person-first language is the norm, see for example the European Association for the Study of Obesity's guidelines on this (https://easo.org/person-first-language-guide-addressing-weight-bias/). Another earlier example of this is with people with AIDS, as early as 1983 the Denver principles argued that "AIDS victims" should not be used instead they should be referred to as people with AIDS.

> **Person first language.** Where we mention the person before the identity group they belong to.

Identity first

However, we can also define people by their identity before the person. This is less common but there are

> **Identity first language.** Where we mention the identity group before the person.

specific groups where this is advocated, arguing that the identity is integral to them as a person. This is seen in autistic, blind and deaf communities. However, within these communities, there is often some debate around using this type of language (see, for example, Vivanti, 2020).

If you are recruiting from specific groups then it is often worth doing a bit of research, looking at charities and advocacy groups to see how best to address people.

Be sensitive

As an overall point, it is worth thinking about how you would like to be talked to when taking part in research.

You should be sensitive to others' feelings. Questions you may find innocuous may trigger emotional responses in others. A simple example is gender; for years surveys would say Gender: Male/Female. Gender is now viewed as more fluid than this, and you will certainly encounter non-binary people over the next few years (if you have not done so already). So, you should consider the response options you give carefully to ensure inclusivity in your research. Indeed, you would want to know if you have recruited this hard-to-reach group after all! Now some people have strong views about this (and I am not about to debate it here!) but even if you have views about how we measure gender, ask yourself is this a hill you want your study to die on? The answer will hopefully be no! Sensitively ask questions and you will maximise recruitment and understand how representative your sample is.

Conclusion

Inclusivity in research is important but often challenging. Hopefully, you can see the problems with the rather narrow (WEIRD) samples that research has been built on, and why this limits our knowledge of psychological phenomena. You will want to try and ensure that you include hard-to-reach groups whenever possible or try to replicate past findings in new populations. Indeed, several research areas would be improved if people attempted to replicate findings in diverse populations. It is also important that you are sensitive to the populations you are studying and address them in the most appropriate way possible as this will improve engagement. Be kind and considerate and you cannot go far wrong, not just in quantitative methods but in everything you do over the next three years of study (which is a nice note to end this book on!).

Further Reading

Gurven, M., Von Rueden, C., Massenkoff, M., Kaplan, H., & Lero Vie, M. (2013). How universal is the Big Five? Testing the five-factor model of personality variation among forager–farmers in the Bolivian Amazon. *Journal of personality and social psychology*, 104(2), 354.

Henrich, J., Heine, S. J., & Norenzayan, A. (2010). The weirdest people in the world?. *Behavioral and brain sciences*, 33(2–3),61–83.

References

Arnett, J. (2008) The neglected 95%: Why American psychology needs to become less American. *American psychologist* 63(7):602–614. [JYC, AF, arJH, PRoc]

Bailey, D. H., Walker, R. S., Blomquist, G. E., Hill, K. R., Hurtado, A. M., & Geary, D. C. (2013). Heritability and fitness correlates of personality in the Ache, a natural-fertility population in Paraguay. *PLoS One*, 8(3), e59325.

Gurven, M., Von Rueden, C., Massenkoff, M., Kaplan, H., & Lero Vie, M. (2013). How universal is the Big Five? Testing the five-factor model of personality variation among forager–farmers in the Bolivian Amazon. *Journal of personality and social psychology*, 104(2), 354.

Hayanga, B., Stafford, M., & Bécares, L. (2023). Ethnic inequalities in multiple long-term health conditions in the United Kingdom: a systematic review and narrative synthesis. *BMC Public health*, 23(1), 178.

Henrich, J., Heine, S. J., & Norenzayan, A. (2010). The weirdest people in the world?. *Behavioral and brain sciences*, 33(2–3),61–83.

Putnick, D. L., & Bornstein, M. H. (2016). Measurement invariance conventions and reporting: The state of the art and future directions for psychological research. *Developmental review*, 41, 71–90.

Mackey, K., Ayers, C. K., Kondo, K. K., Saha, S., Advani, S. M., Young, S., ... & Kansagara, D. (2021). Racial and ethnic disparities in COVID-19–related infections, hospitalizations, and deaths: a systematic review. *Annals of internal medicine*, 174(3), 362–373.

Raleigh, V. S. (2022). Ethnic differences in COVID-19 death rates. *BMJ*, 376.

Robertson, E., Reeve, K. S., Niedzwiedz, C. L., Moore, J., Blake, M., Green, M., ... & Benzeval, M. J. (2021). Predictors of COVID-19 vaccine hesitancy in the UK household longitudinal study. *Brain, behavior, and immunity*, 94, 41–50.

Segall, M. H., Campbell, D. T., & Herskovits, M. J. (1966). *The influence of culture on visual perception* (Vol. 310). Indianapolis: Bobbs-Merrill.

Vivanti, G. (2020). Ask the editor: What is the most appropriate way to talk about individuals with a diagnosis of autism?. *Journal of autism and developmental disorders*, 50(2), 691–693.

Index

For Product Safety Concerns and Information please contact our EU
representative GPSR@taylorandfrancis.com
Taylor & Francis Verlag GmbH, Kaufingerstraße 24, 80331 München, Germany

www.ingramcontent.com/pod-product-compliance
Lightning Source LLC
Chambersburg PA
CBHW070323270326
41926CB00017B/3740

9 781032 612386